KARATE STREET SURVIVAL

Fumio Demura & Dan Ivan

EMPIRE BOOK/AWP LLC
Los Angeles, CA.

DISCLAIMER

Please note that the author and publisher of this book are NOT RESPONSIBLE in any manner whatsoever for any injury that may result from practicing the techniques and/or following the instructions given within. Since the physical activities described herein may be too strenuous in nature for some readers to engage in safely, it is essential that a physician be consulted prior to training.

Revised Edition published in 2024 by AWP LLC/Empire Books. Copyright (c) 2024 by AWP LLC/Empire Books.

All rights reserved. No part of this publication may be reproduced or utilized in any form or by any means, electronic or mechanical, including photo- copying, recording, or by any information storage and retrieval system, without prior written permission from AWP LLC/Empire Books.

Revised edition Library of Congress Catalog Number:

ISBN-13: 978-1-949753-72-1

24 23 22 21 20 19 18 17 16 15 14 13 12

Library of Congress Cataloging-in-Publication Data

Karate Street Survival by Demura Fumio and Ivan Daniel -- ed. p. cm.

ISBN 978-1-949753-72-1 (pbk. : alk. paper) 1. Martial arts-- technique. 3. Large type books. I. Title. GV1114.3.F715 20713261.815'3--dc22

20060101981

Printed in the United States of America.

KARATE STREET SURVIVAL

Fumio Demura & Dan Ivan

Table of Contents

Preface
Self Defense, 7
    Defense Against Holds, 8
    Defense Against Punches, 26
    Defense Against Kicks, 32
    Defense Against Club, 36
    Defense Against Knife, 41
    Defense Against Multiple Attacks, 48
    Defense Against Pistol, 52
Tactics and Strategy, 55
    Defensive Postures, 56
    Sitting Defense, 58
    Unusual Situations, 59
    Using a Weapon for Defense, 60
    A Closer Look at Your 'Body Weapons' and How to Use Them, 64
Apprehension Restraint, 71
    Police Apprehension, 72
Karate, 87
    Punching, 89
    Stances, 92
    Karate Strikes, 94
    Kicking, 98
    Blocking, 104
    Karate Sparring, 112
Aiki-do, 121
Judo, 133
    Throws, 134
    Chokes, 141
    Falls, 145
Exercises, 147
Psychological Strategies against Attack or Rape, 150
    Defense against Attack, 150
    Types of Assailants, 151
    Do's and Don'ts for Prospectie Victims, 152
    Defense against Rape, 154
    Acknowledgement
Dan Ivan, 160
Fumio Demura, 162

Preface

The necessity for self-defense seems to be very real. One need only to listen to the daily news or read his local papers to realize that these are violent times. The degree of violence to which you are exposed depends on the area in which you live. Naturally, the war zone of the Middle East, or the slums of a big city, are dangerous environments. But even he who lives in a typically peaceful law-abiding midwestern town is susceptible to some form of violence. It may be nothing more than an irate drunk taking a swing at you, or, to use a more extreme example, it could be a drug-crazed youth with knife. Although this may sound like an alarmist attitude, we are stating the facts of the situation, a view supported by the experts and statistics. These are supposed to be modern and civilized times, and we do have the finest police officers in the world to protect us. Keep in mind though, a criminal, mugger or attacker does not make his move in full view of a policeman or witnesses. They choose a time and place in which you, the average citizen, are the most vulnerable. There has been, we have noticed, a rather remarkable growth in the popularity of martial arts in the world in the past few years, including Karate, Judo, Kung-fu and many others. This is an indication that people everywhere are searching for a little extra confidence, some added protection for themselves and their families. Mankind centuries ago invented and refined combative arts for the same reason they exist now, self-defense. We recommend, if it is available to you, to take a course in Karate or one of the other martial arts. If you are presently doing so, this book will be a supplement to your training. However, if you are among the great number of men and women who haven't the time or facilities to learn self-defense, this book is definitely for you. The most common and frequent attacks you may encounter are covered, from simple grabs to attacks with weapons and by groups. Included are chapters on essential techniques of Karate, Judo and Aiki-do directly related to learning street self-defense. In the chapter on Tactics you may learn to avoid an attack altogether or at least have an advantage in unusual situations. An added feature is a very important contribution on the subject of rape by two prominent psychologists. Any woman studying this book may find invaluable information on rape-preventive measures in this section. As instructors holding degrees in various fighting arts, we have assembled the most effective and practical techniques and information possible, techniques that you can realistically learn and use, we hope, to make you a 'survivor' in the streets, not a 'victim'.

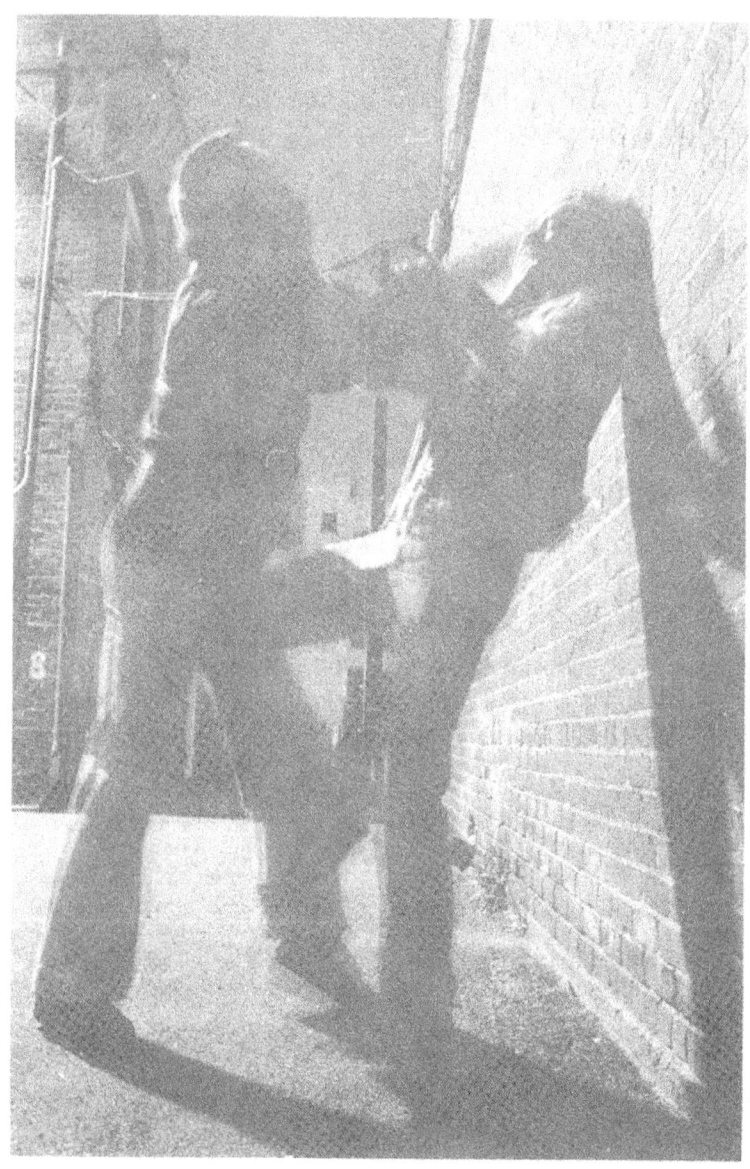

Self-Defense

For self-defense in the street to be effective, it must be simple and direct. The examples offered in this manual have been carefully chosen. We have purposely omitted any difficult moves such as fancy kicks to the head, intricate holds and difficult throws that require hours of professional training to master. What you will study here are actually suggestions for defensive action applicable to a wide variety of situations, since no one can accurately predict what an attacker will do. We have given you our honest appraisal of these situations based on years of experience in the streets and as instructors to civilians, police and the military.

An important fact is that emergency situations do not allow time to think or remember complex defense measures. Therefore, as a rule of thumb, one should go for the EYES, THROAT AND GROIN. Even an amateur can cause excruciating pain and do very serious damage at these locations.

Throughout this book, the use of knees, elbows and open finger attacks prevails. This is because we have found that a novice or untrained man or woman can counter attack more effectively with these moves. If you are a Karate expert, then a single, well-placed punch or kick may dispose of an opponent. But this manual is concerned with the average man or woman who is trying only to survive. Each attack illustrated gives a series of counters to apply. The purpose of this is to stimulate your imagination, and all the techniques are interchangable.

You are not expected to remember precisely whether to kick your opponent or gouge his eyes when time is of the essence. In an emergency we recommend you defend with the first thing that comes to mind at any opening. Then follow up until the attacker is completely defeated.

USE COMMON SENSE! Many attacks do not call for drastic action. A simple punch or shove may discourage the attacker, especially if he is an unruly friend or perhaps a drunk neighbor that you have no need to harm. DON'T TAKE ANY CHANCES WITH STRANGERS. We advise you protect yourself no matter how trivial or insignificant the aggressive act might seem. Many serious incidents have resulted from a simple nudge with the shoulder or a minor traffic accident. Always use whatever force is necessary.

To be more effective in blocking, hitting, and kicking, study the section on Karate. To master the chokes and throws better, study the section on Judo. To learn simple restraining or pressure moves, study the section about police or Aiki-do. Don't expect to escape from a fight totally unharmed. Prepare yourself mentally to accept pain and still fight back. Even experts get hurt in fights but this must be overcome in order to counterattack and survive.

Defense Against Holds

Attacks from the Front

This section deals with attacks or grabs from the front. One who approaches from the front is usually exposed to a kick. This is normally sufficient to ward off an attack. However we have added a variety of counterattacks so that you can increase your repertoire of self-defense moves.

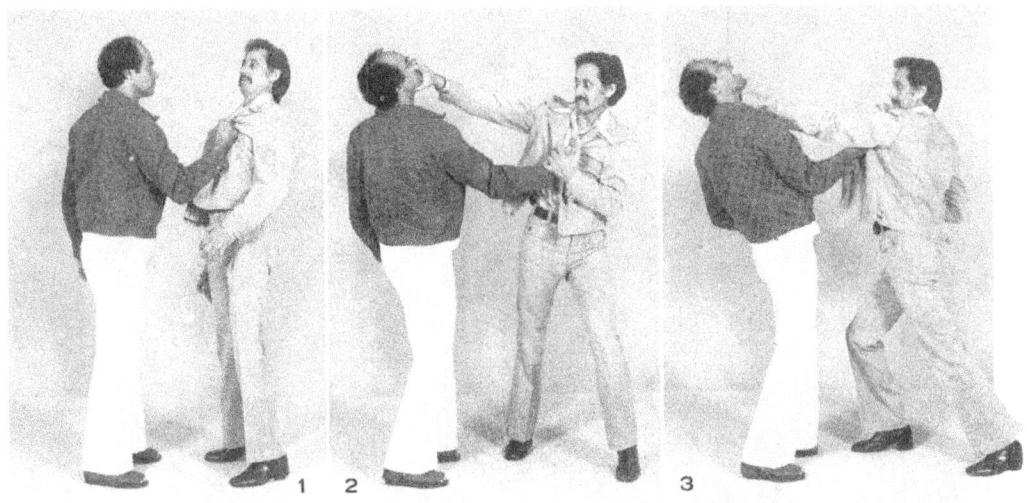

1. Lapel grab:
2. Twist sideways to avoid a punch from the other hand.
3, 4, 5. Thrust your hand toward his face and gouge. Follow up with whatever techniques are necessary.

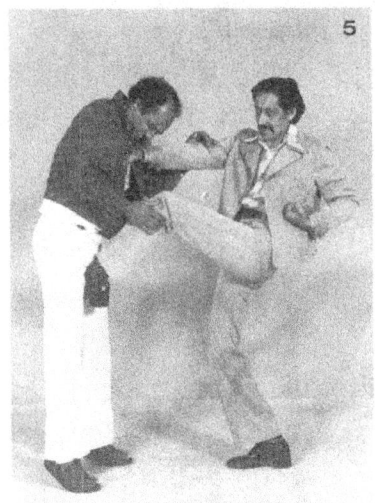

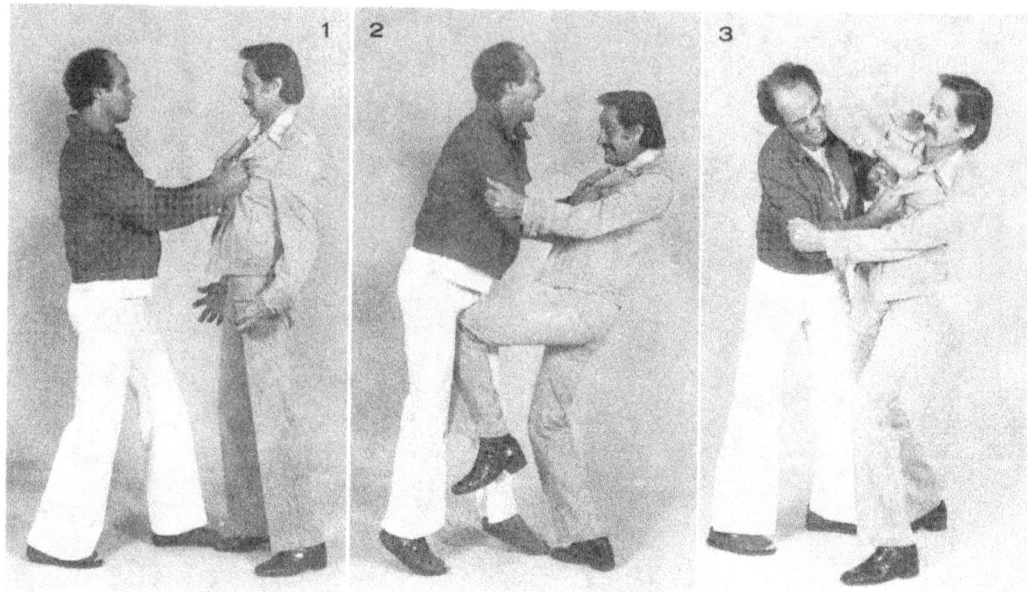

1. Two-hand lapel grab:
2. Grasp his arms and pull toward your knee.
3. Follow up with elbow strike.
4, 5. Follow up until attacker is defeated.

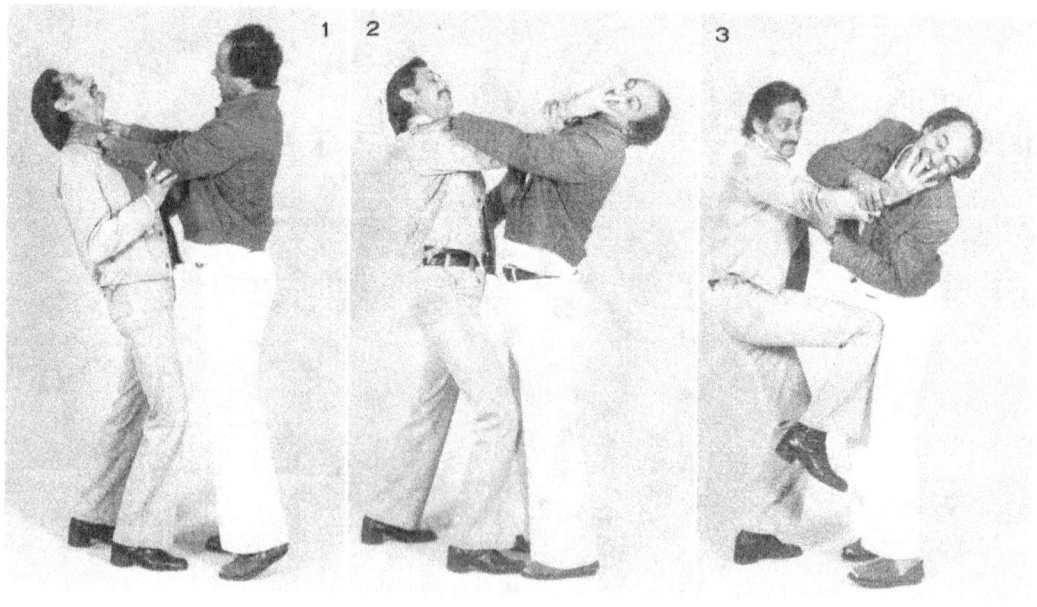

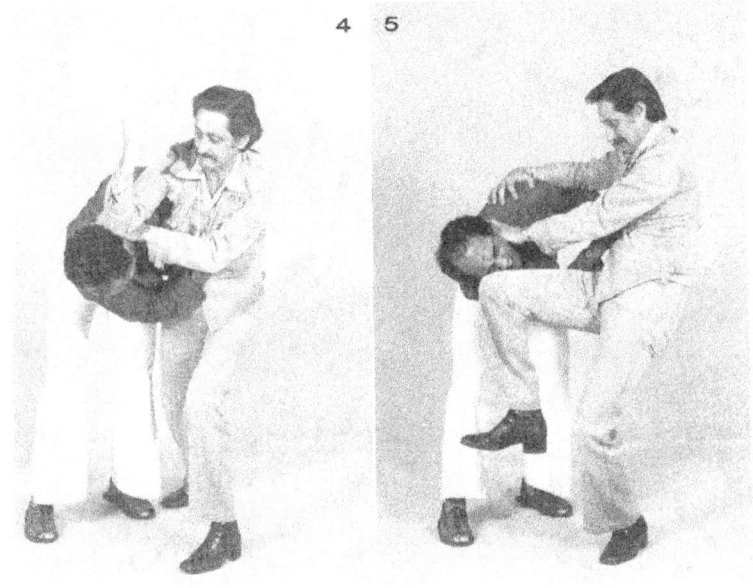

1. Choke:
2. Gouge at throat or eyes.
3. Simultaneously bring knee to groin.
4, 5. Follow up.

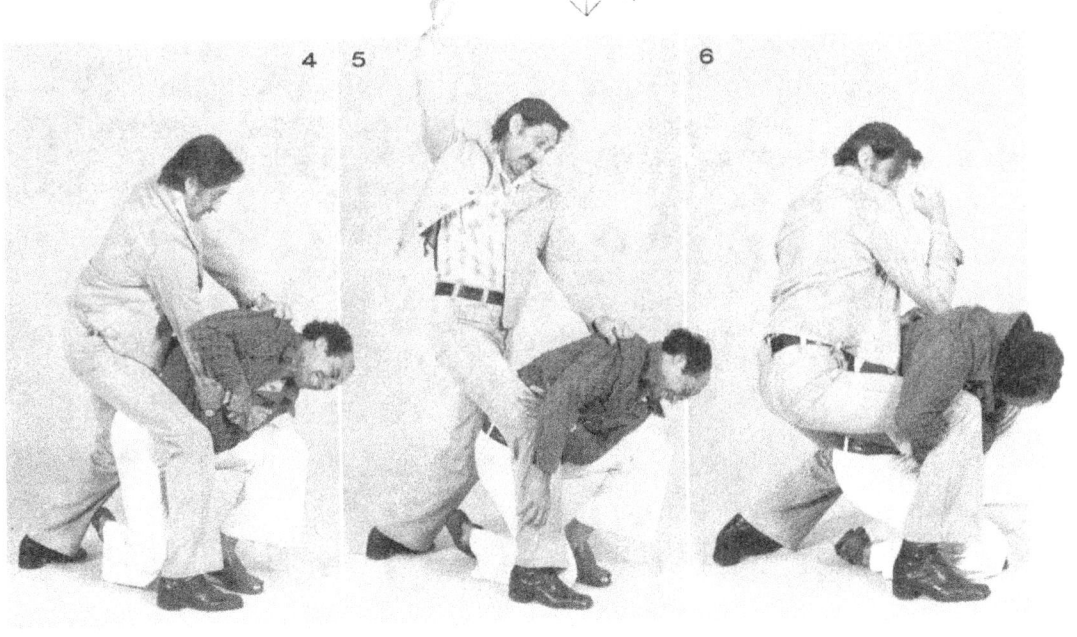

Karate Street Survival

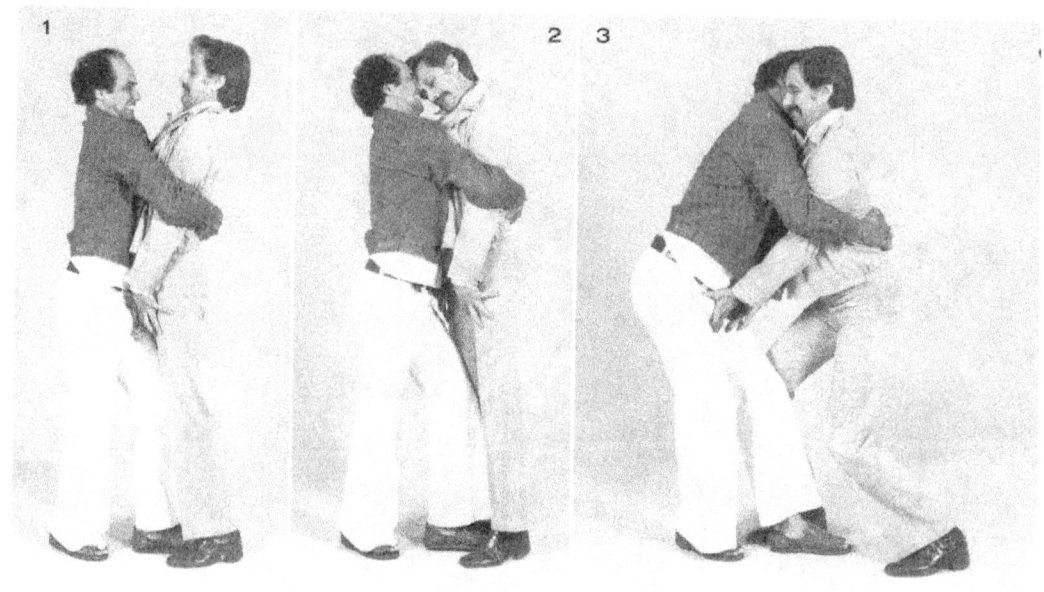

1. Two-hand wrist grab:
2. Kick groin, pulling him toward you.
3. Pull hands free.
4. Chop to head or neck.
5. Follow up.

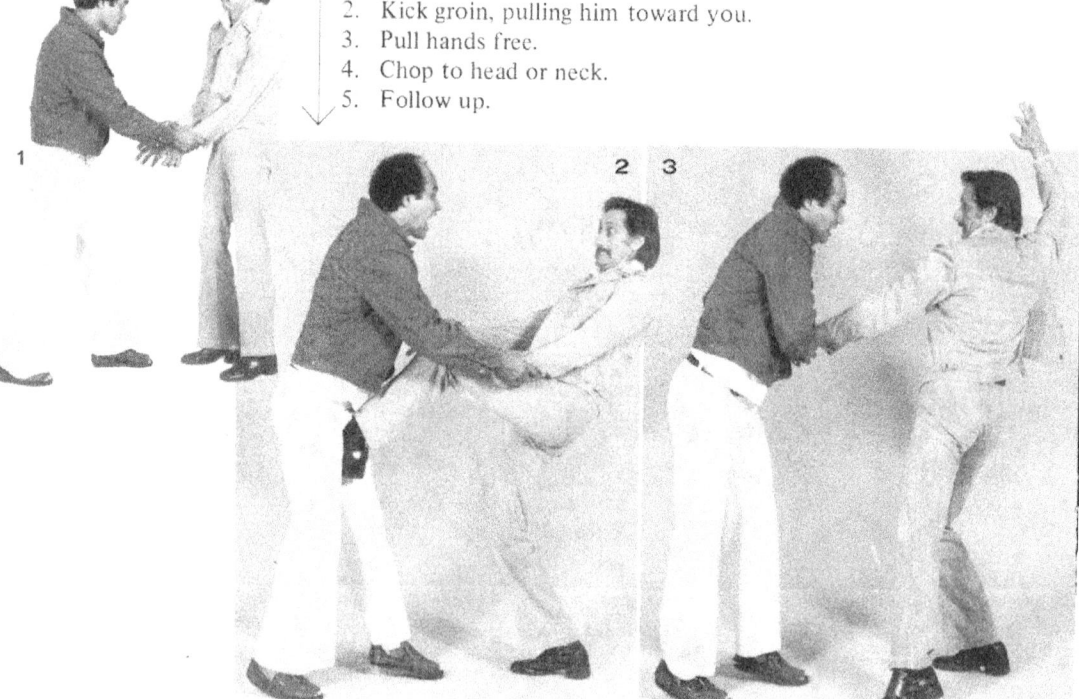

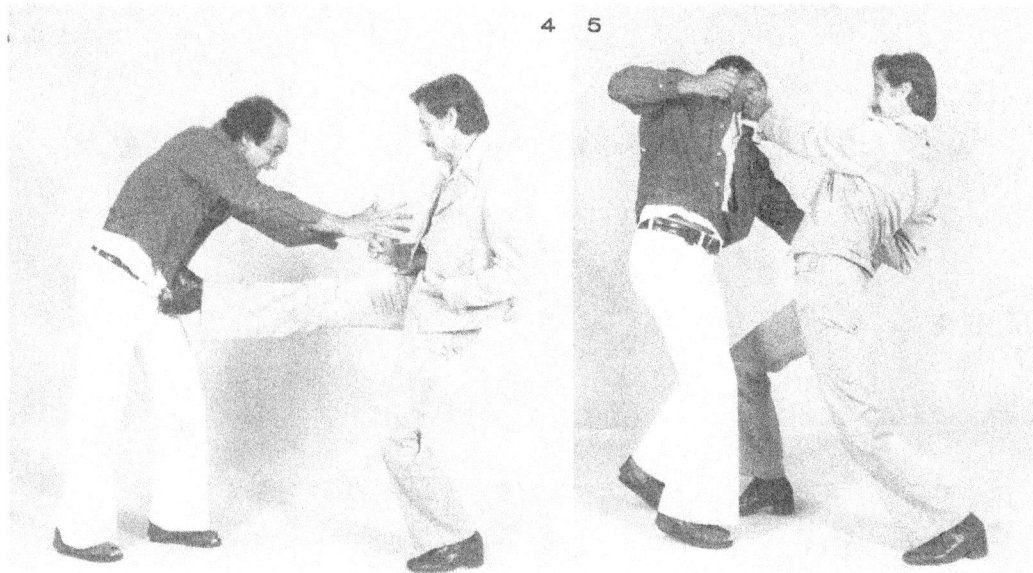

1. Body grab:
2. Head butt (knee to groin).
3. Strike or grasp groin.
4. Break free and kick.
5. Follow up.

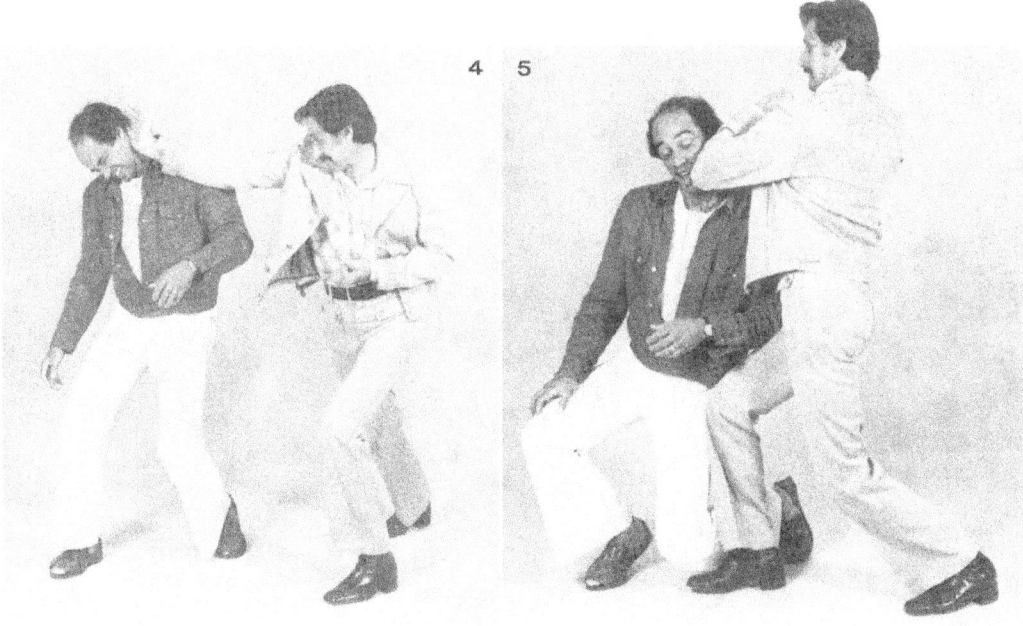

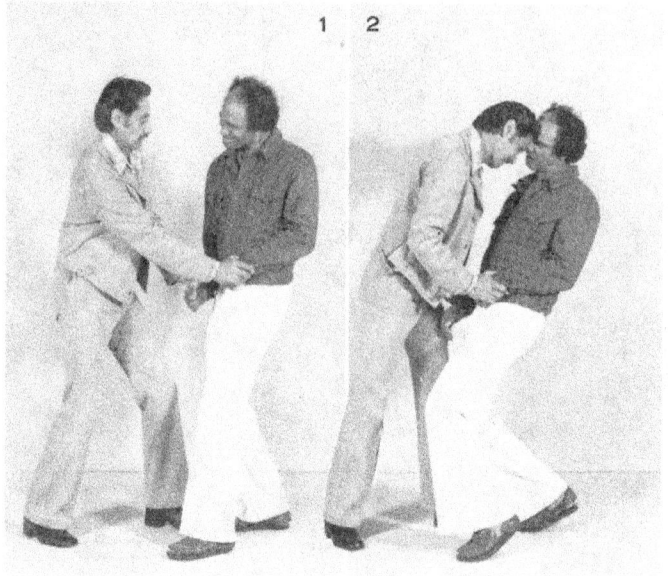
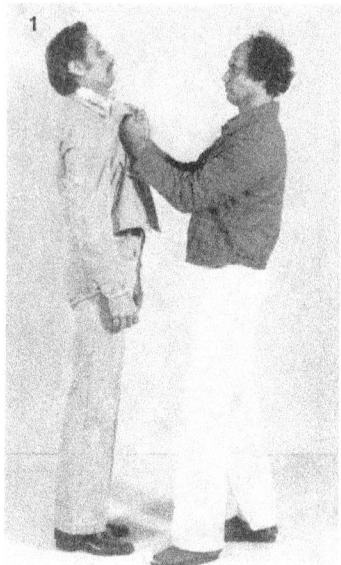

1. Before he attacks:
2. When close in, grasp arms and pull into a head butt. In this instance you take the initiative and attack.

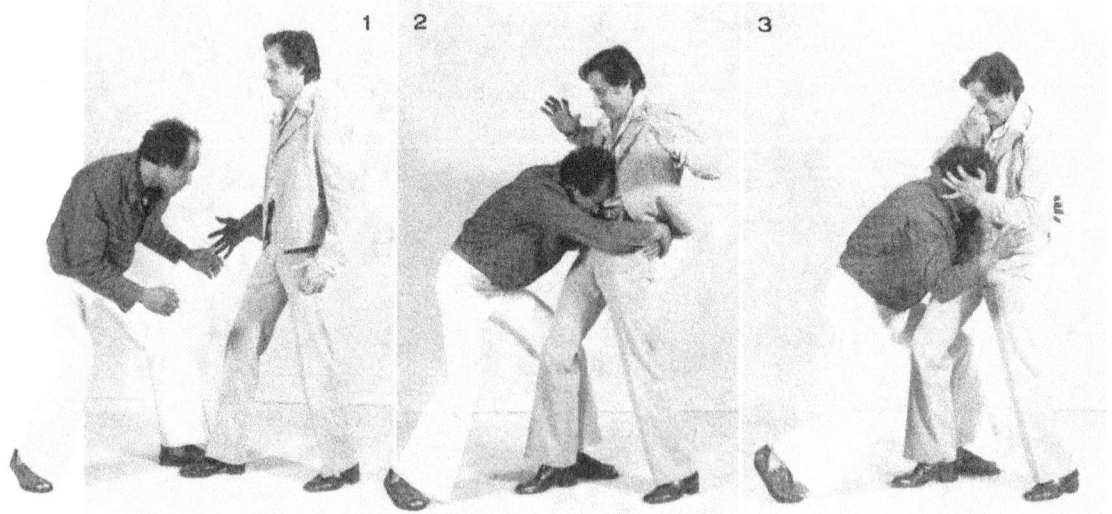

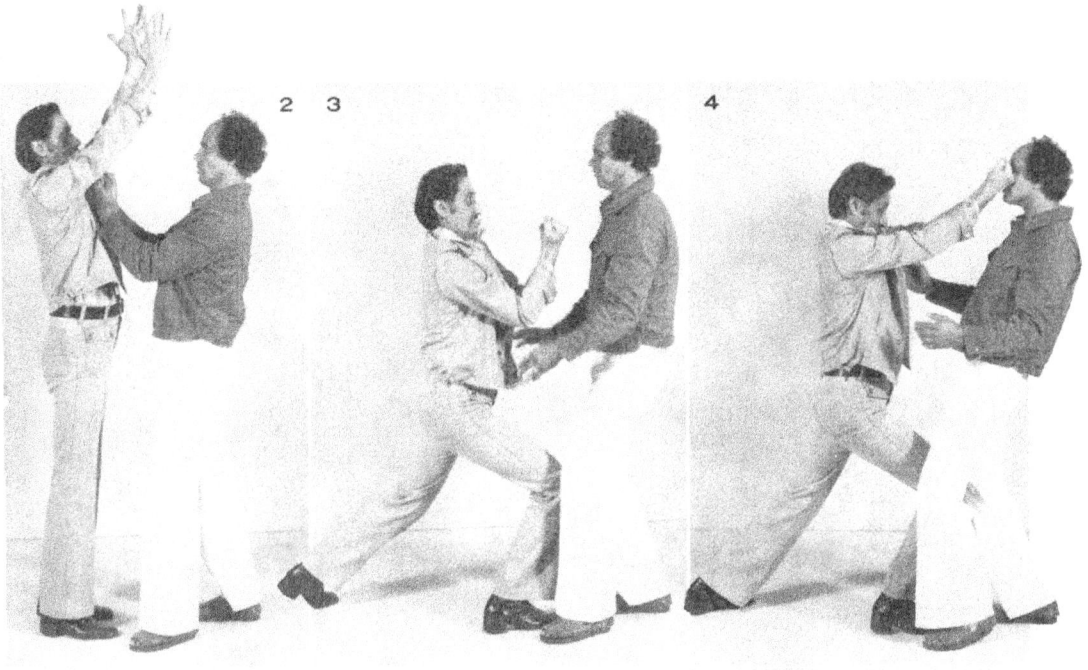

1. Two-hand lapel grab.
2. Lift your arms up high.
3. Shift your weight back and bring elbows sharply down on his arms.
4. With continued motion, thrust both fists into face and eyes.
5. Following up with your knee is easy.

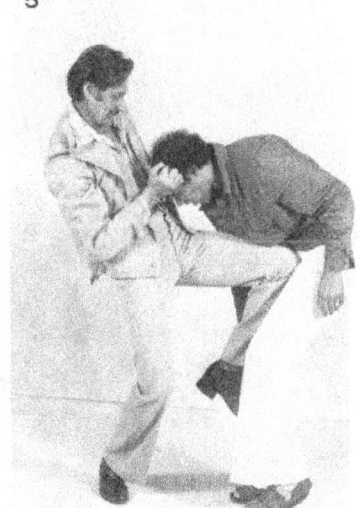

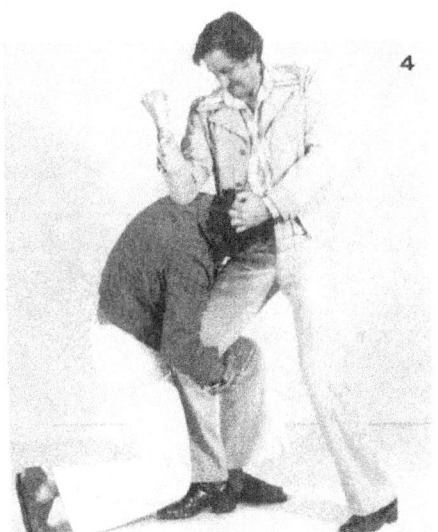

1,2. Lunge and grab body.
3. Slap both palms against ears.
4. Follow up.

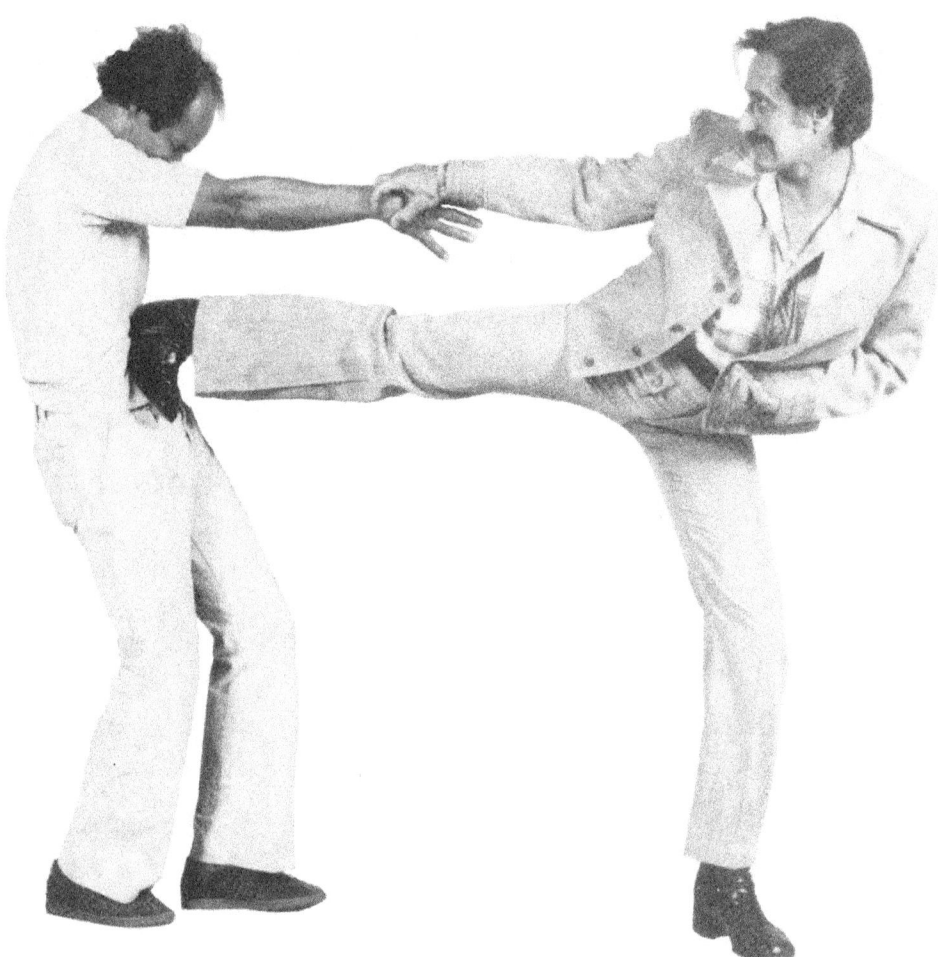

Attacks from the Side
Broadsiding (catching someone unaware from the side) is a favorite method for bullies. You can effectively defend without turning toward the attacker. This section will teach you the proper response to this type of attack.

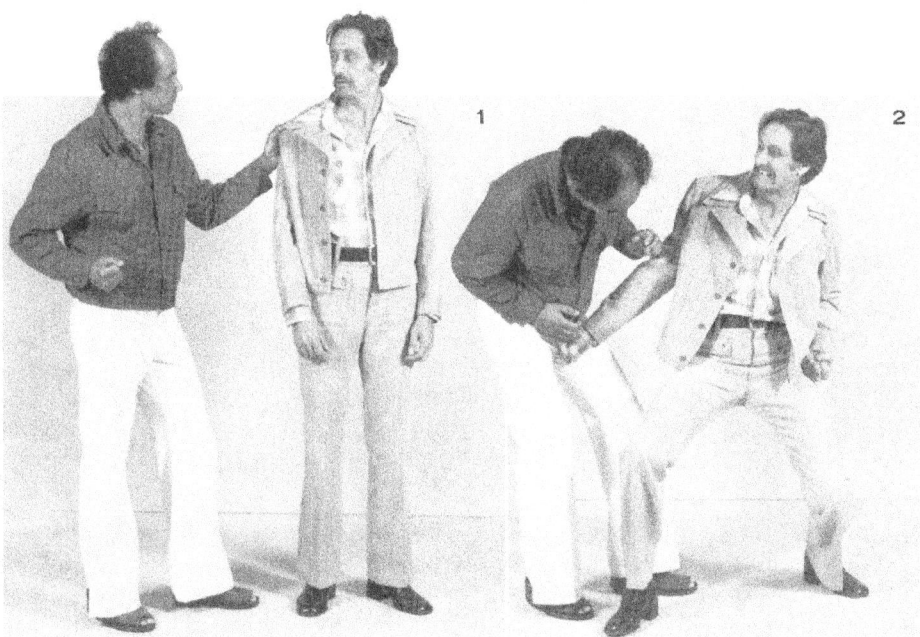

1. Grabbing shoulder:
2. Snap the back of your fist to his groin.
3. With a continuation of your motion, snap the fist into his face as he bends from the groin blow.
4. Turn toward your attacker and follow up.

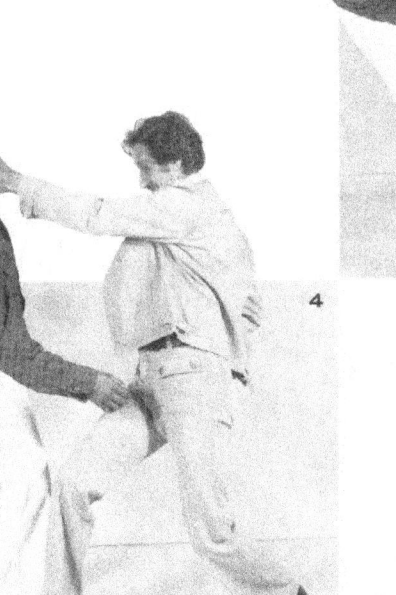

Karate Street Survival

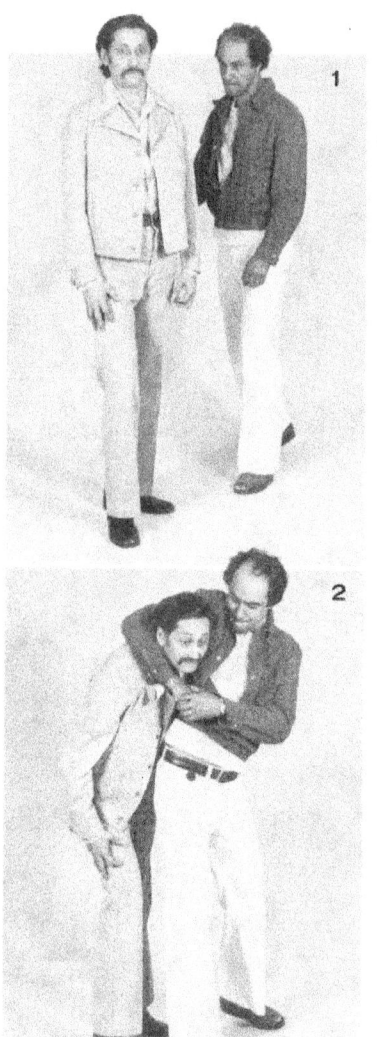

1. Headlock:
2. Punch his groin with your free hand.
3. Pull free and move up behind.
4. Step on his leg at the knee joint to bring him to the ground.
5. A choke or blow can then be excuted.
6. Follow up.

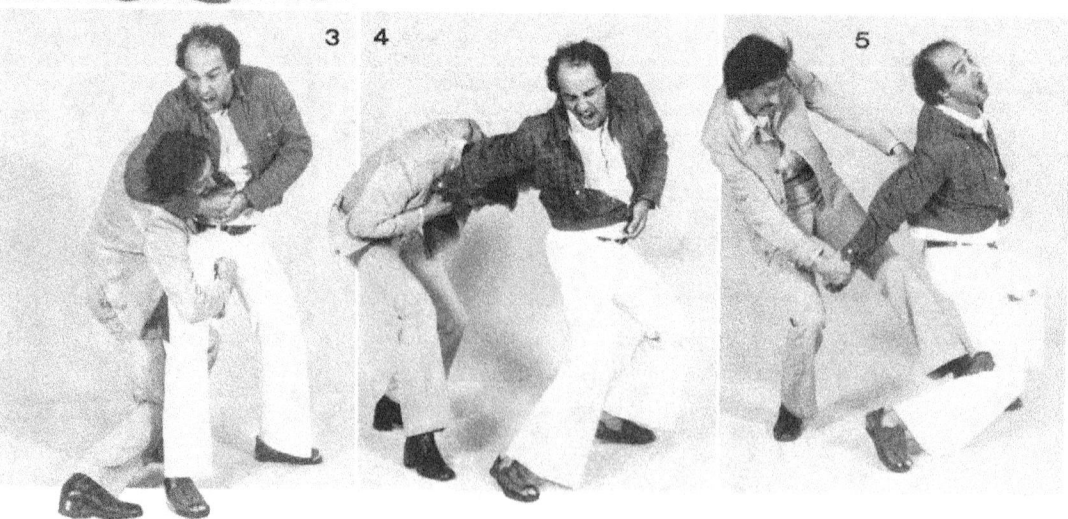

1. Arm grab from side:
2. Execute side kick to shin or knee.
3. Pull free after kick.
4. Bring elbow to face.
5. Follow up.

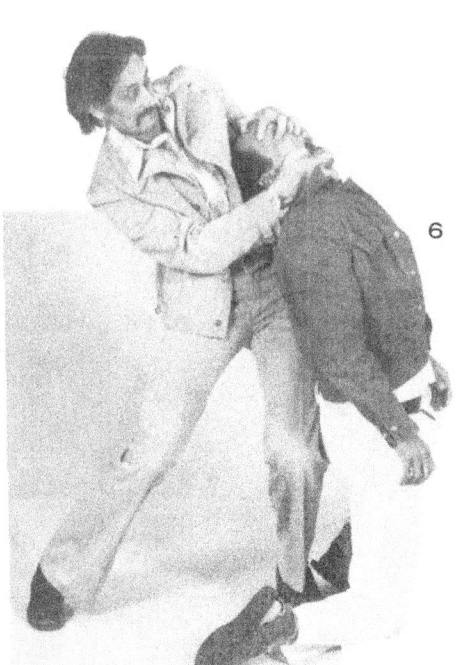

Attacks from the Rear

When someone grabs you from the rear he usually employs both arms. This leaves your legs or sometimes both arms and legs free. Many counters are possible, but it is best to try to develop back kicks and learn to strike to the rear.

1. Full nelson:
2. Drop your body weight and grope for his face and eyes with fingers.
3. Execute heel stomp to instep or leg.
4. Follow with elbow smash to face.
5. Turn and follow up.

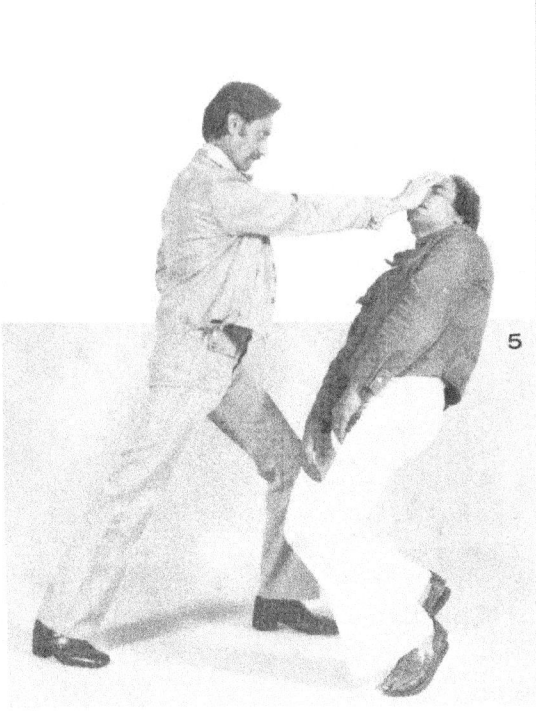

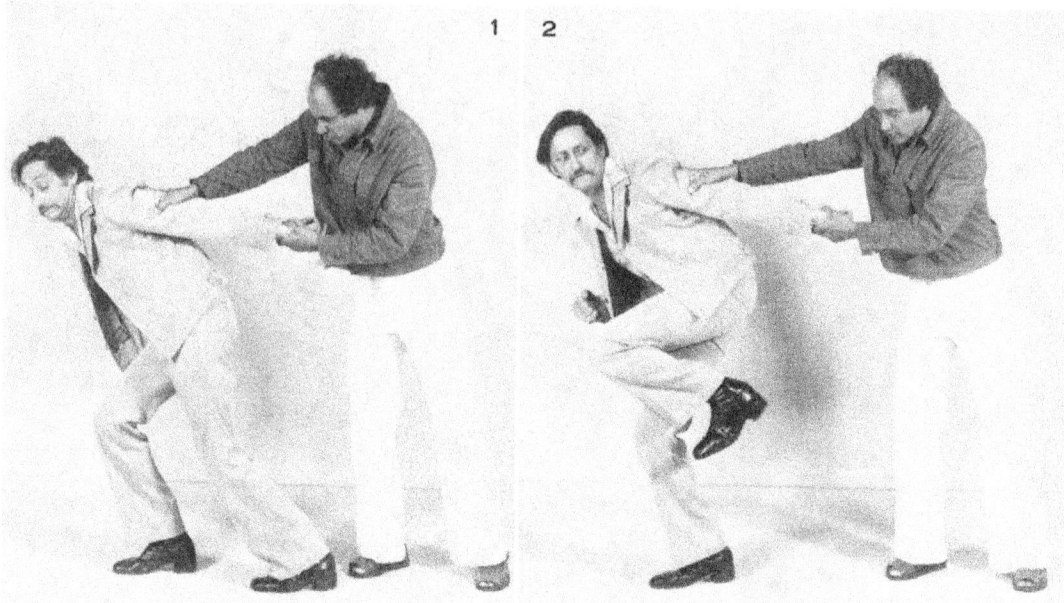

1. Rear arm grab:
2. Raise leg for back kick.
3. Kick back toward groin.
4. Follow up.

Note:
Even if your arm is fully extended you can reach someone with your legs. You may have to shift your weight and balance to reach him but respond quickly and look over your shoulder at the attacker, and it can be done.

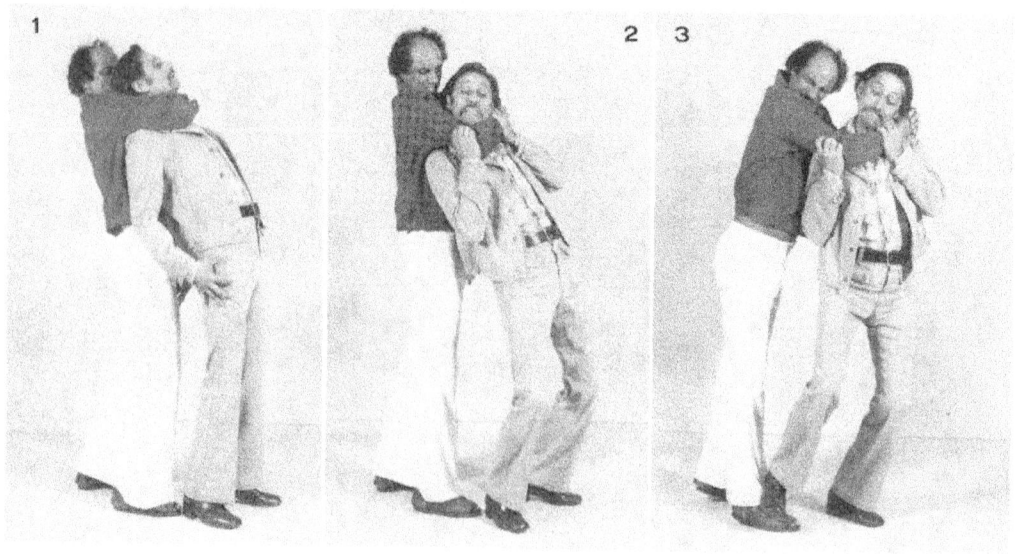

1. Rear Choke:
2. Turn head quickly to relieve pressure on your windpipe.
3. Simultaneously stomp on his foot.
4. Execute an elbow smash to the ribs.
5. Pull him over the leg and throw him to the ground.
6. Follow up.

Note:
When choked you must react quickly before opponent sets himself and cuts off your wind. Speed is essential.

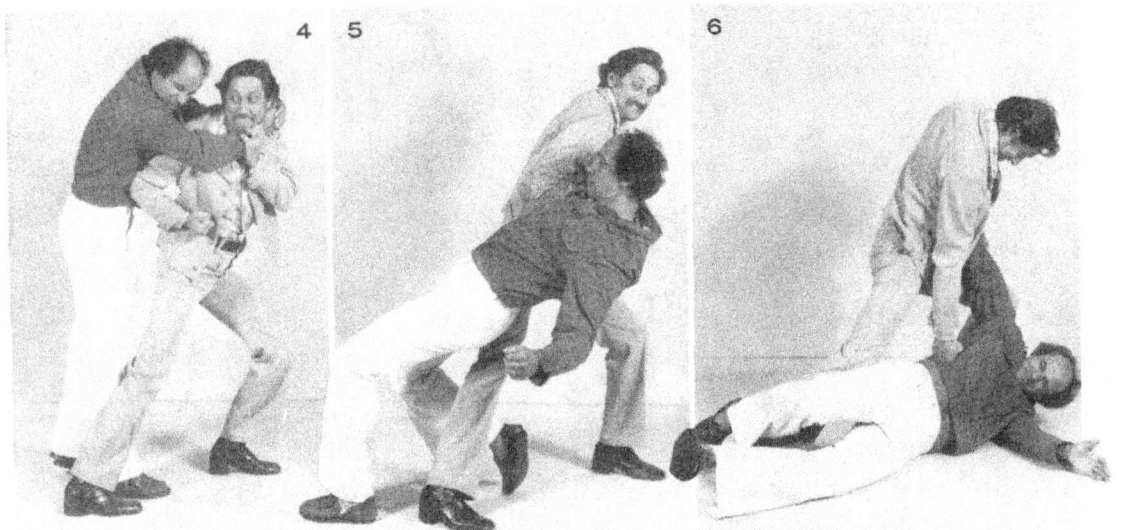

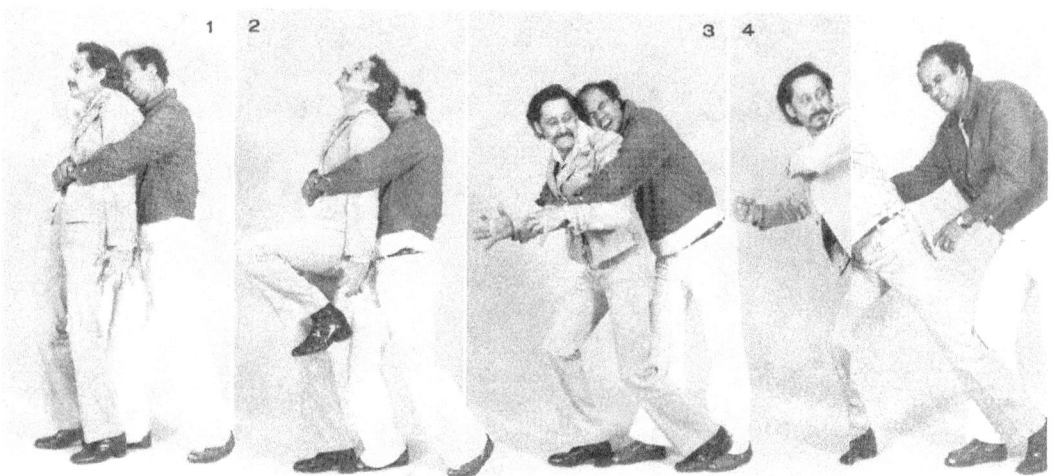

1. Body hug from rear:
2. Use a head butt if possible.
3. Stomp on his foot with your heel.
4. Break free quickly.
5. Follow with an elbow smash to face or chest.
6. Follow up.

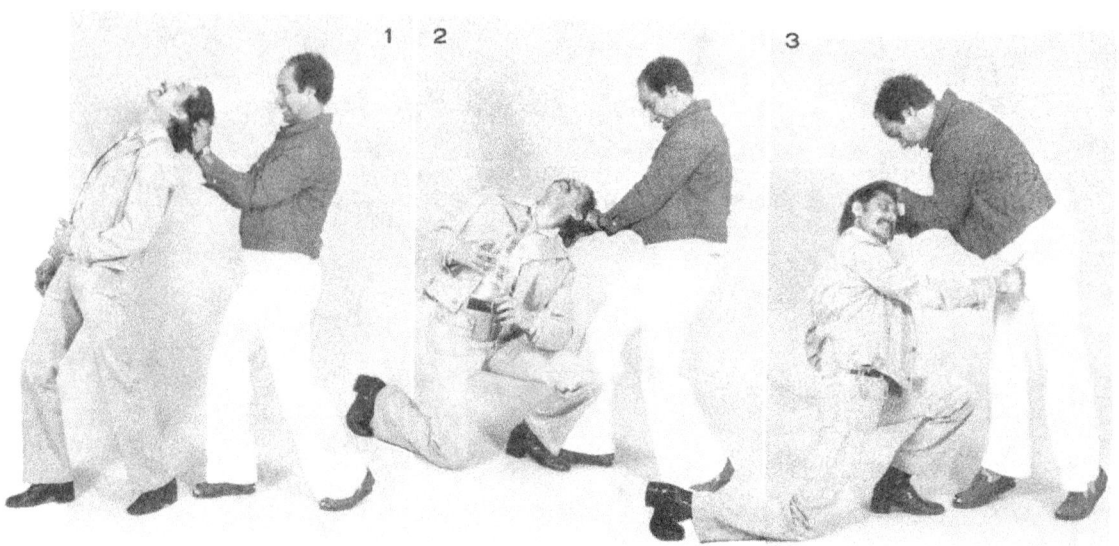

1. Pulling down from behind:
2. Turn while dropping to your knee for balance. Keep your hand out for protection against his legs.
3. Punch or strike groin.
4. Go for the throat with a clawing grab.
5. Quickly get back to your feet.
6. Follow up.

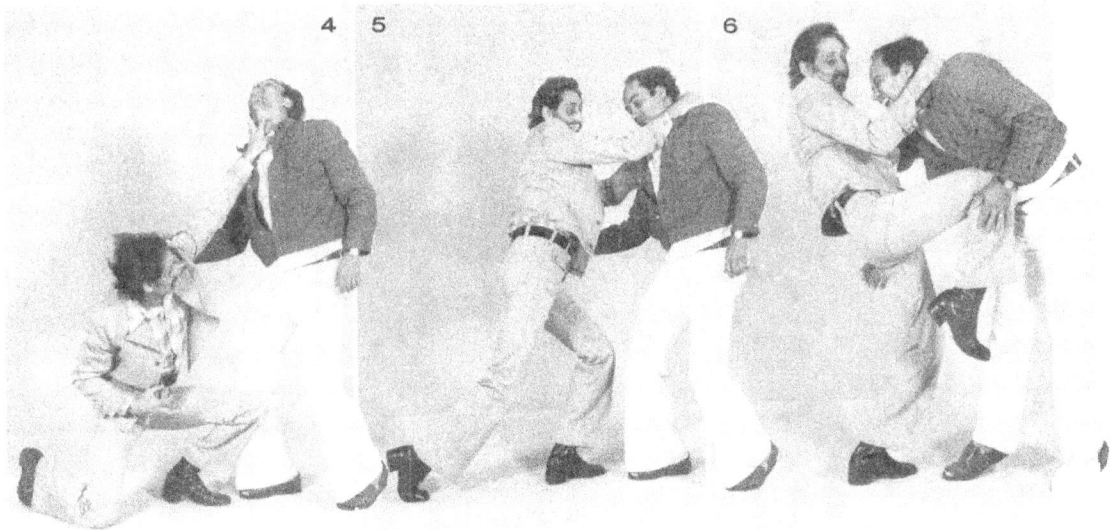

Defense Against Punches

Possibly the hardest set of techniques to learn are for blocking punches because they require very quick reactions. If you watch an attacker closely, you can anticipate the punch. There is generally an inhalation or some preparatory motion that can be detected. The average man will draw the fist back or lift it up, sometimes even twisting the body to take a bigger swing. Observing this gives you time to prepare or even counter before the punch reaches you.

Concentrate on your opponent's face and eyes to read his motion. Always draw back a step while executing a block. In this way you brace yourself and reduce some of the power of the punch. *Study the karate chapter to improve your blocking ability.*

1. Sweep block: Using the open hand to sweep punches aside is one of the most natural ways to avoid getting hit.
2. Quickly counter before your opponent can throw a second punch.

Sweep block. Pulling back and to the side. This reduces the power of a punch if it is coming at you in a circular fashion. Block with your palm and quickly chop with the same hand.

Bottom:
Backhand sweep block. Raise your arm and use the back of the open hand to ward off the punch. Draw back, brace, and counter-kick.

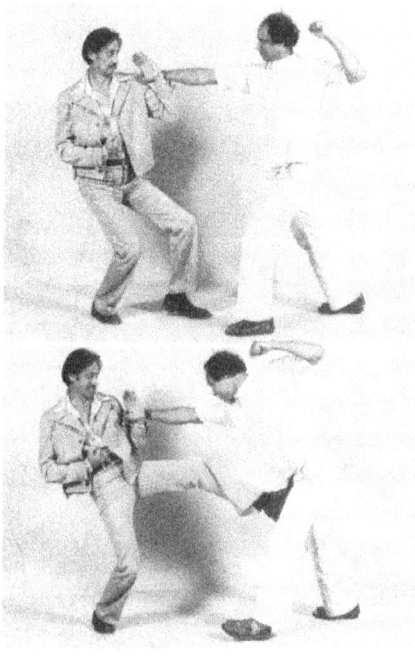

1. Inside forearm block:
2. Use the arm closest to the opponent (in this case the blocking arm) and go for his eyes. *Impair his vision.*
3. Application of your palm heel to his chin will snap his head back.
4, 5. Follow up.

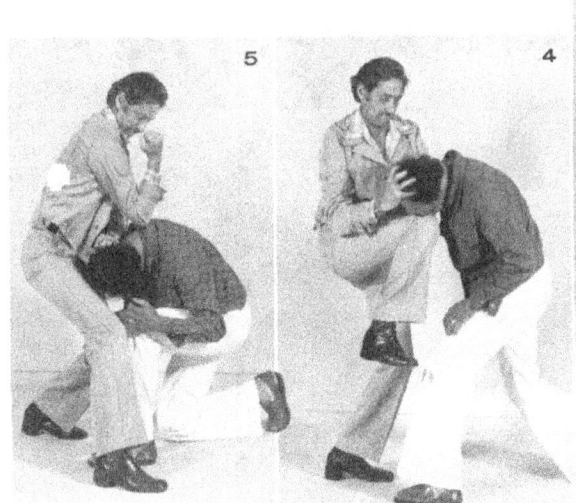

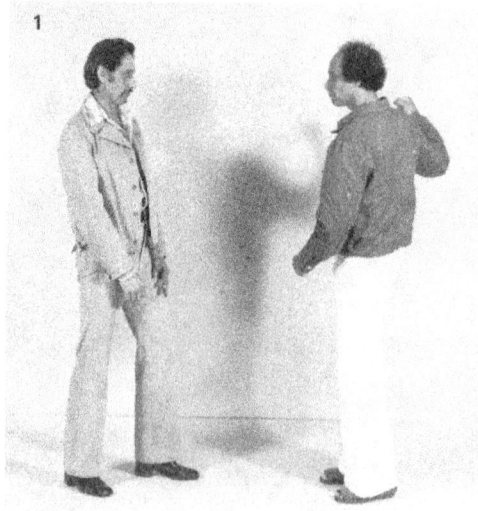

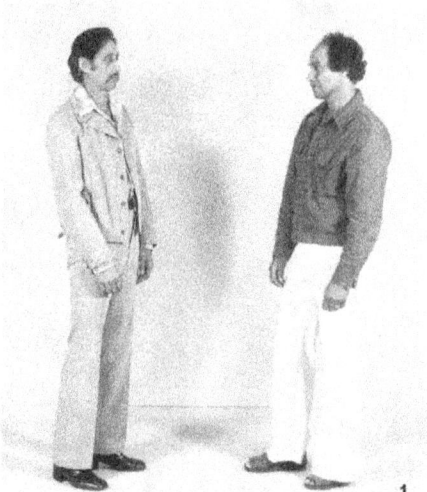

1. Stomach punch:
2. Use the forearm block. Keep arm down and swing it across the body while pulling away.
3. Counter quickly. The example here is an extended knuckle to the eye to impair vision.
4, 5. Follow up.

1. Upward block:
2. Thrust your forearm upward as shown against face punches or overhand blow.
3. Slide in with elbow blow to chest.
4. Follow up.

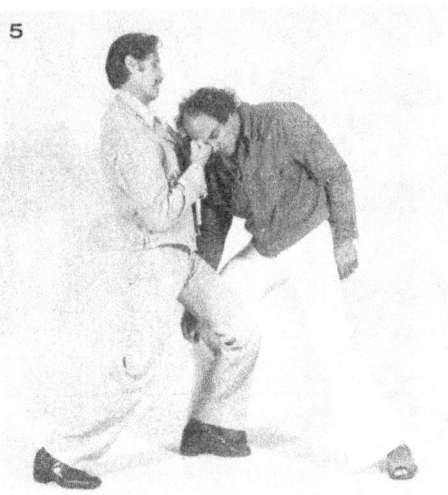

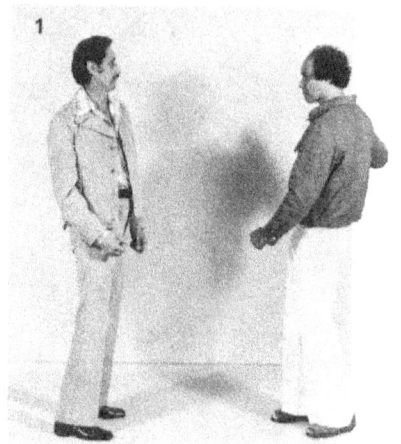

1. Straight punch:
2. Employ the forearm block again, this time pulling around into side stance. This block is used frequently and has the most force to damage your opponent's arm.
3. Slide in and under arm with blow directed toward groin.
4. Bring elbow across head.
5. Here is an example of bringing opponent to ground.
6. When down, finish off adversary to be safe.

1. Straight punch:
2. Once again use the forearm block using the hard bone surface of your arm. Swing from outside, inward and across body.
3. Counterchop to his face with the same hand.
4, 5. Follow up.

1. Arguing stage:
2. To make a point here, you can react as soon as you anticipate trouble. Kick to the groin even before, or while, the punch is being thrown.
3. Always follow up aggressively.

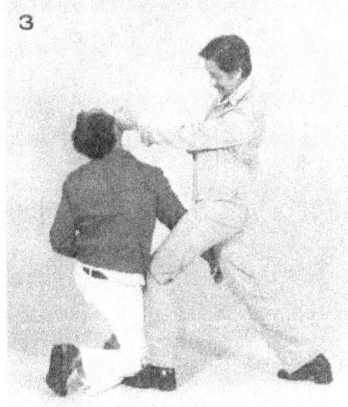

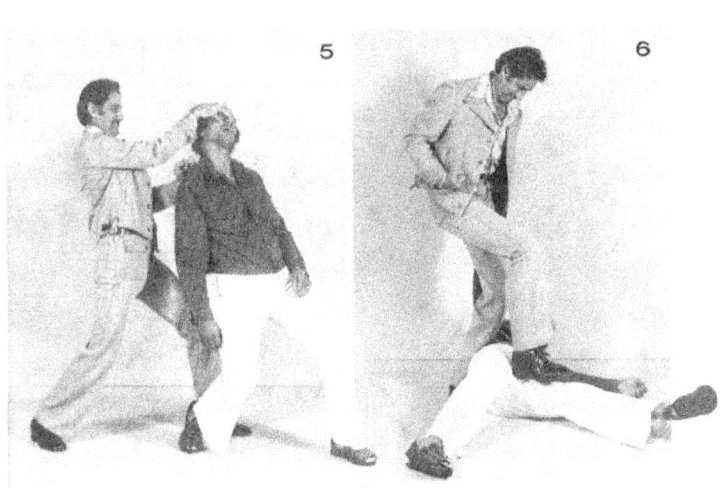

Defense Against Kicks

This is not as difficult as it may seem, because untrained persons cannot usually put enough force or snap into the kick. In addition to the blocks shown here you can also TWIST THE BODY TO AVOID CATCHING THE KICK ON THE GROIN. Turning sideways and letting the kick hit your leg will cause less pain and damage than the groin or stomach. Our chapter on Tactics discusses how to use a weapon of some kind to drive off an attacker.

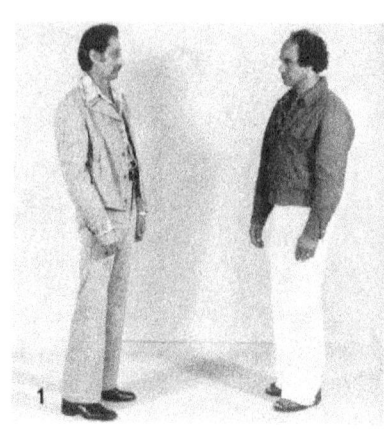

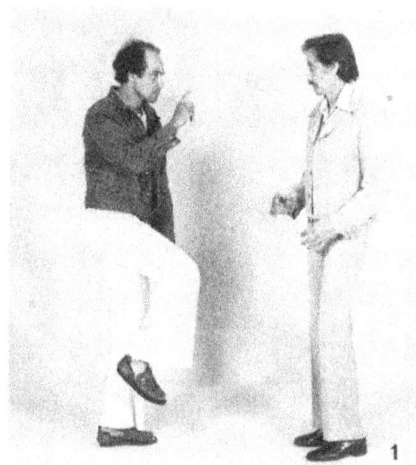

1. Front kick defense:
2. Dodge sideways away from the kick. Block with your arm, pushing the kick away from your body.
3. As your attacker expends his power and drops forward;
4. Counterkick to his extended leg at the knee joint.
5. When he buckles, slide in for a chop to the neck.
6. Finish off with an elbow.

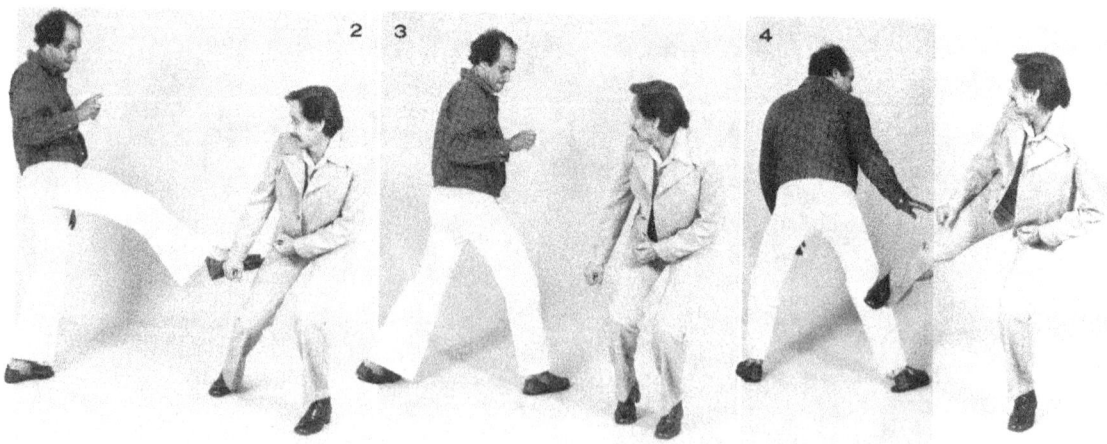

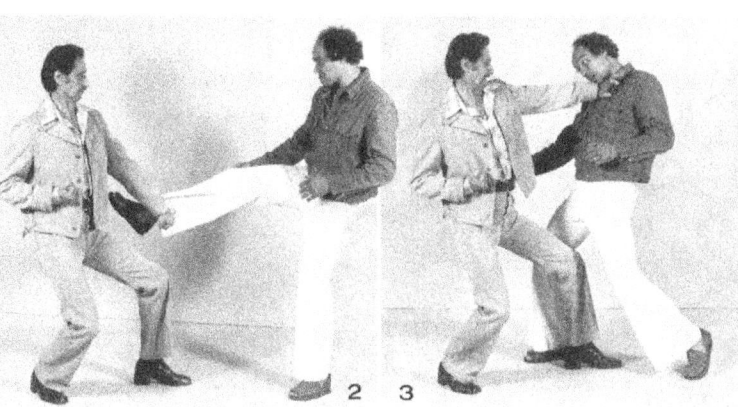

1. Front kick:
2. Use a *downward block* by hitting at the leg with your arm and deflecting it to the outside.
3. As his leg expends its forward momentum counterchop to neck (remember to pull back and away from kicks).
4, 5. Counterkick and follow up.

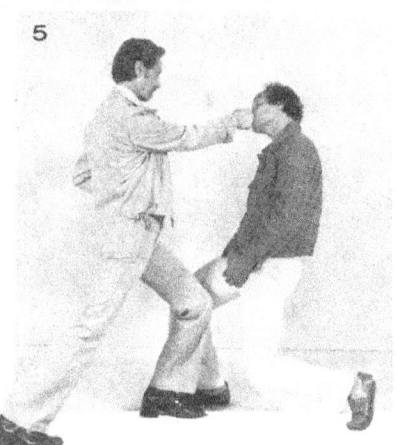

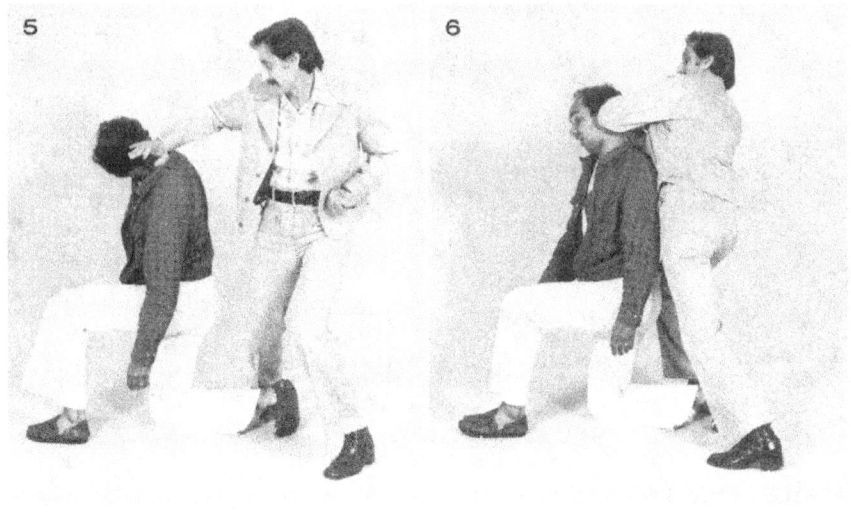

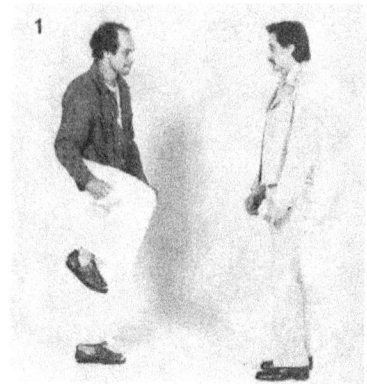
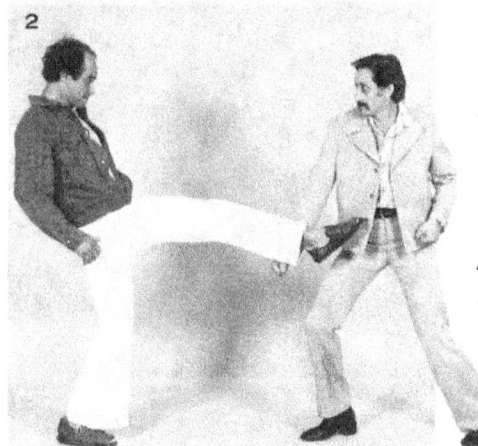

1. Front kick defense:
2. With your forearm, sweep his leg to the inside.
3. Simultaneously, draw back and away from the kick.
4. Counter chop (or backhand blow).
5, 6. Follow up.

1. Kick defense:
2. Shift back completely out of range. Crouch and prepare to counterkick.
3. Keep your arms in front of you for added protection. REMEMBER IT WOULD BE BETTER TO CATCH A KICK ON THE ARMS THAN IN THE GROIN OR STOMACH.
4. Sliding in to reach him, if necessary, counter front kick to groin.
5, 6. Follow up.

Note:
Shifting in and out, judging distances properly and balancing your weight are very important for counterkicks. Study the chapter on Karate.

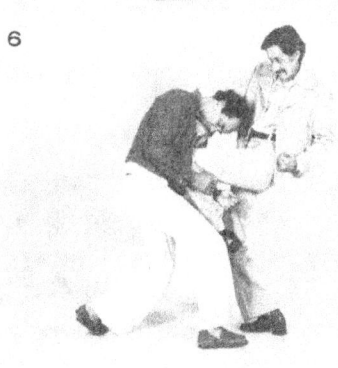

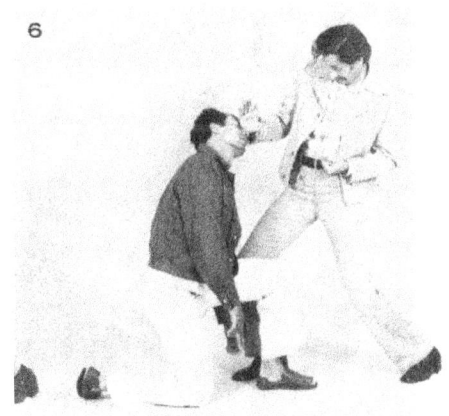

Defense Against Club

The photograph shows a man taking a club blow on the arms. The point is that it is better to sacrifice your arms than your head. Even a small or physically weak person can hurt you seriously or cause death with a club. Grab any kind of counter weapon you can. Read closely the section on Tactics.

1. Club attack:
2. Before your opponent swings the club is the best time to react. Kick to vital targets as hard and frequently as necessary.
3. Follow up until the attacker is completely disabled.

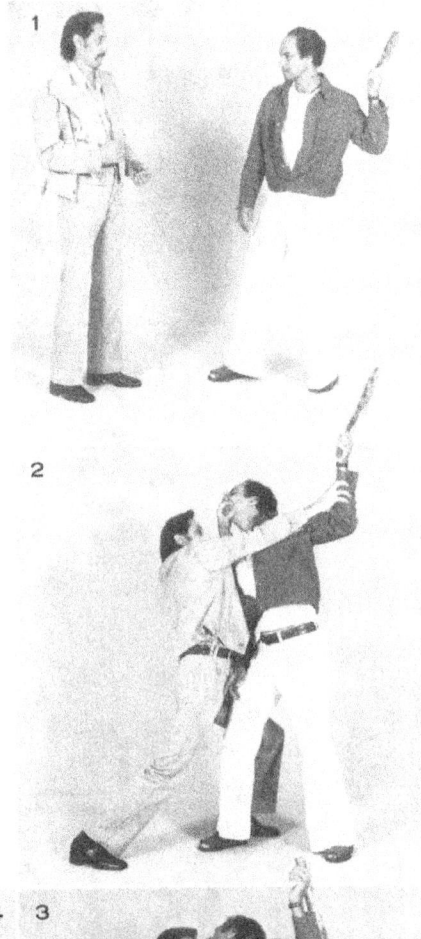

1. Preparing to attack with club:
2. When you see opponent raising a club or preparing to hit you, ACT FIRST. If close enough, slide in and check his arm, at the same time going for his eyes.
3. Bring your knee to the groin hard, fast and repeatedly.
4. Claw and rip at the throat with your hands. Follow up.

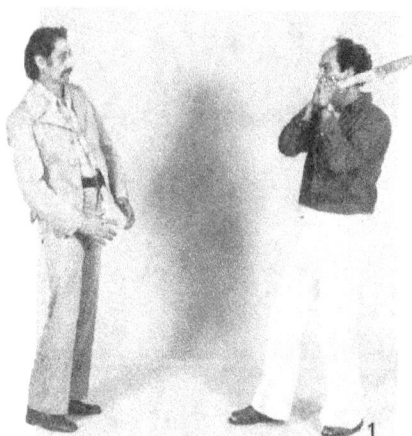

1. Circular body blows may be the hardest to block:
2. Catch the blow on your arms rather than your body.
3. Counter with kicks.
4, 5. Follow up attacks.

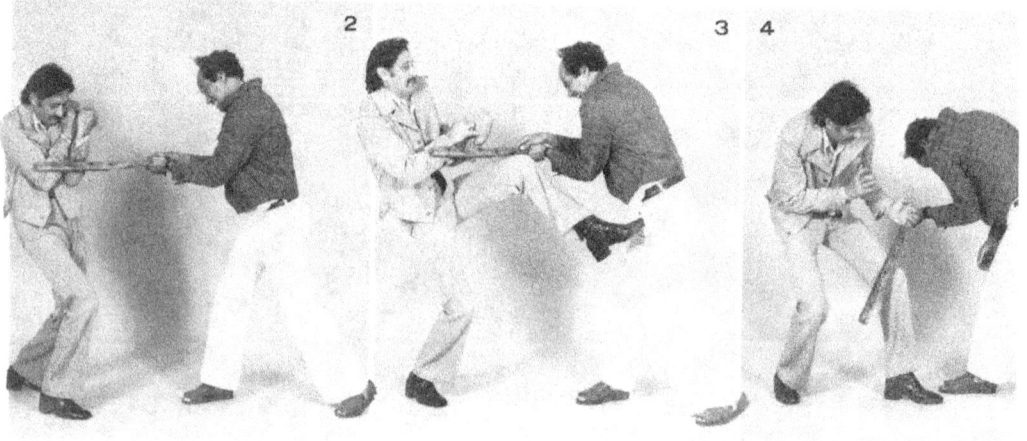

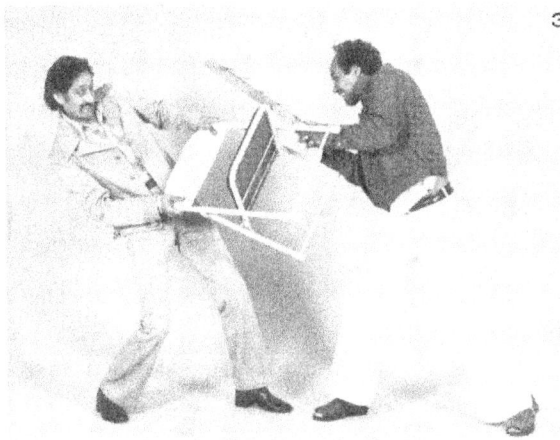

1. Counter with a weapon:
2. A chair, for example, might be handy. When your attacker grabs a club, you grab a chair.
3,4,5,6. This self-explanatory sequence will give you some idea of how to use a counter weapon of some kind.

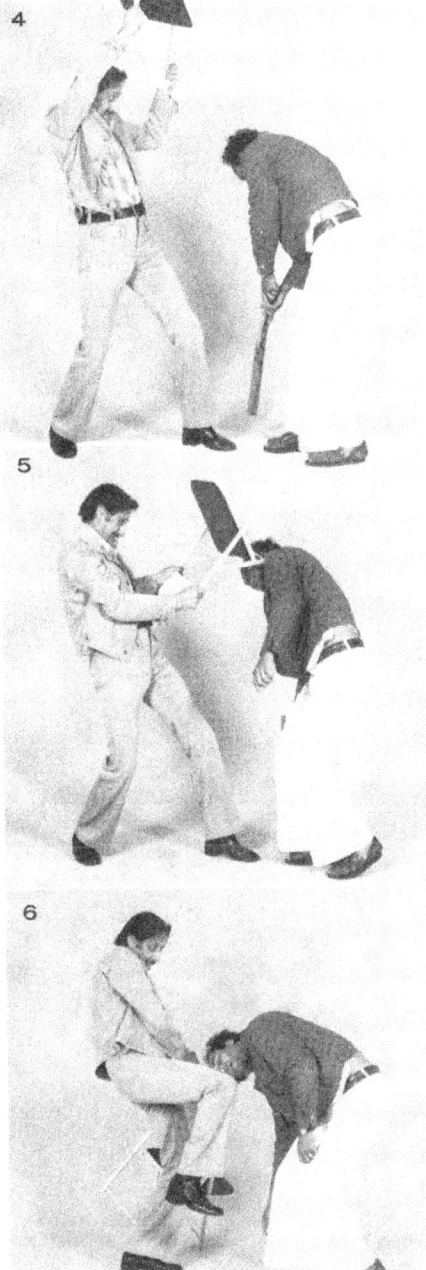

1. Dropping under a powerful club blow:
2. For an overhand blow from which you don't have time to escape, or should you fall or slip to the ground, follow this sequence.
3. Keeping your hand up for added safety, drop and kick at his legs.
4. Follow up kicks and rise from the ground quickly.

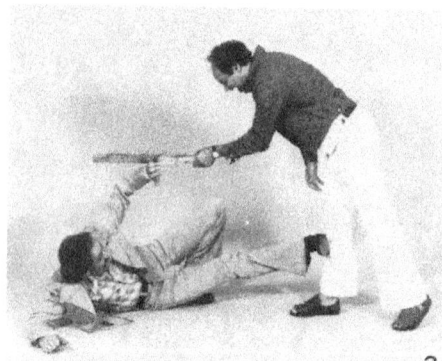

Note:
Dropping to the ground is a last resort. Stay on your feet if at all possible.

Defense Against Knife

Here we are dealing with life and death situations. If you cannot *run* or *get away*, fight with some kind of weapon. Use your legs as much as possible to keep your body away from the knife. As a last resort, catch the knife on the arms, hands or legs rather than the body or head. Even if injured, you must fight back. Men with knife wounds and even those bleeding profusely can survive. Fight viciously only if absolutely forced and you cannot get away.

Bottom illustrations:
1. Example of how to deflect a knife with your shoe sole.
2. Example of kicking at knife or at hand holding knife.

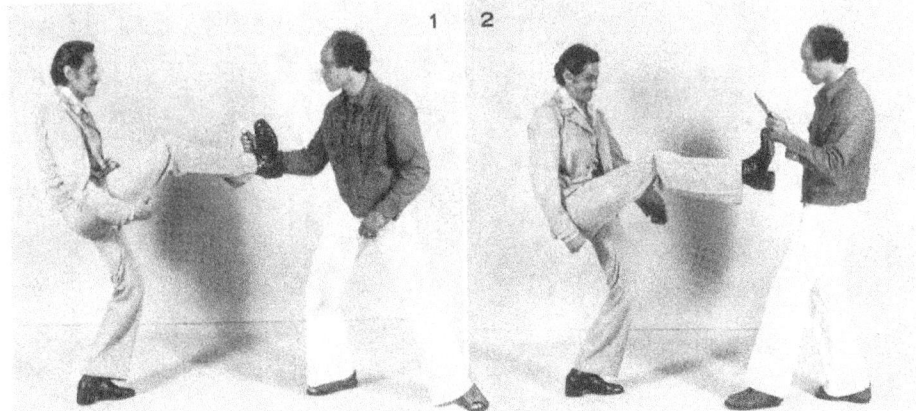

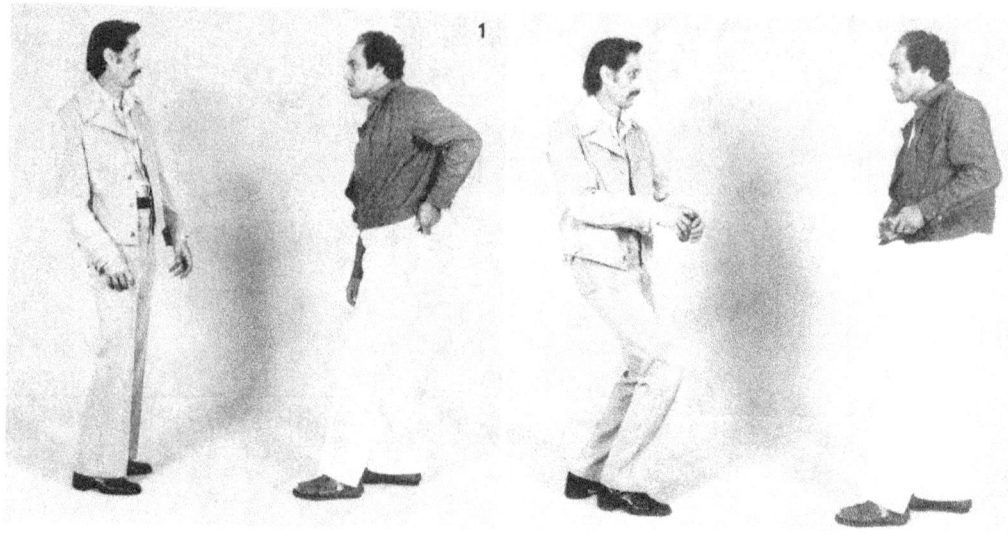

Below sequence of knife defense:
Illustrates how you might use your belt buckle to counter.

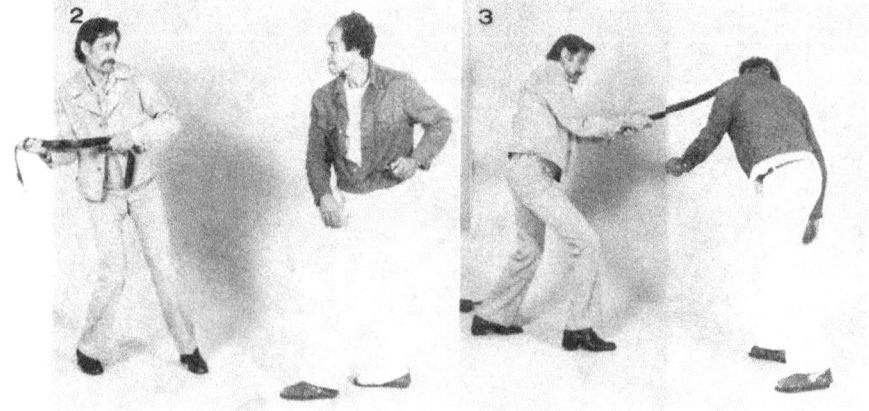

1. Drawing a knife:
2. *Act first* when you see your opponent reaching for a knife.
3. Kick toward his groin, staying out of reach as much as possible.
4. Go for the eyes and follow up any way you can to insure your safety.

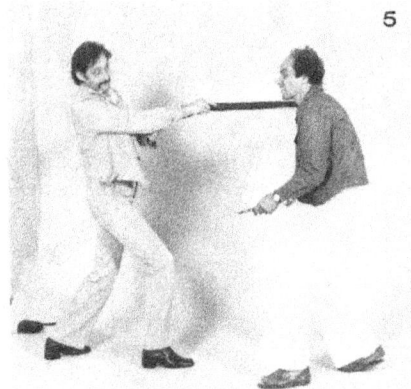

1. Knife attack:
2. When opponent prepares to attack, take something from your pocket.
3. Throw keys, pocket change, even your wallet at opponent's eyes to distract him.
4. Follow this distraction up with kicks or other attacks.

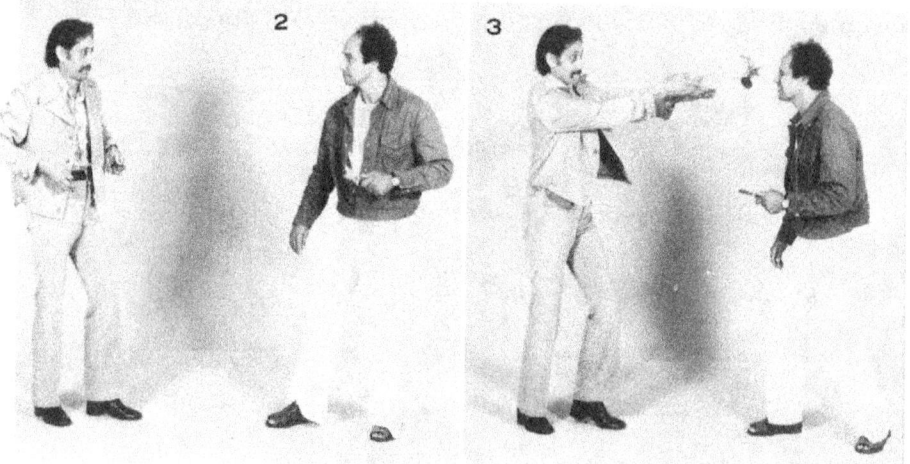

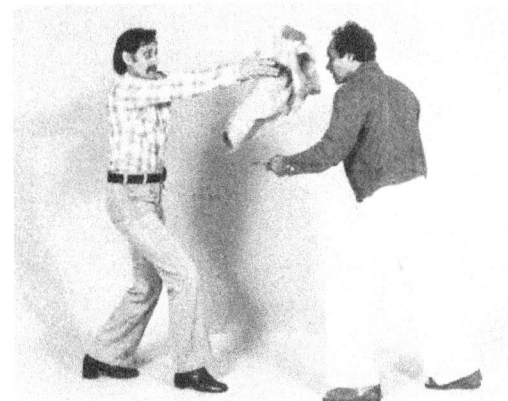

Alternate sequence of knife defense: Illustrates how you might throw some clothing at opponent if time permits you to get it off. *Wrapping an item of clothing around an arm to fend off slashes with the knife can also be considered.*

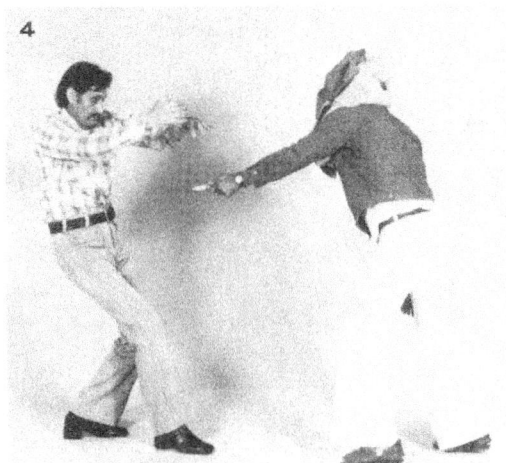

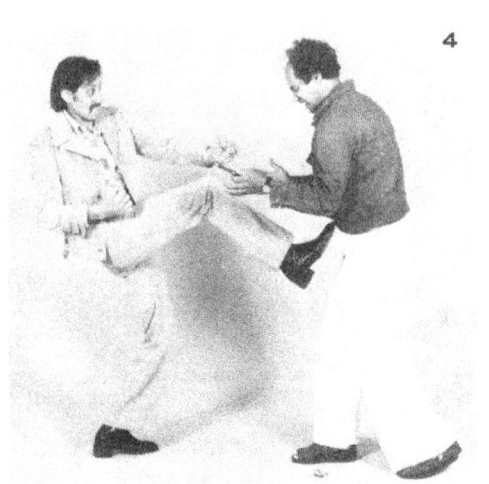

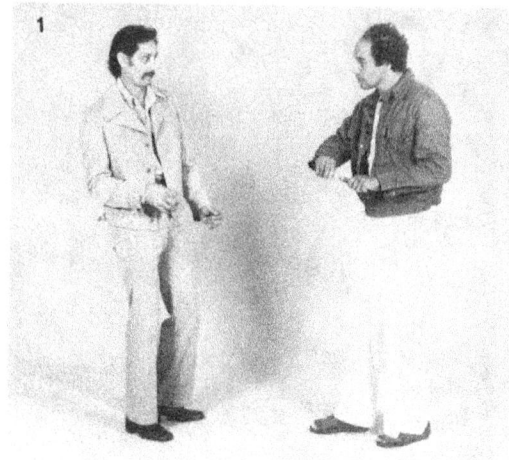

1. Lunge attack with knife:
2. It is safest to keep your distance, but if you are caught by surprise and don't have time to pull away, parry the thrust with your hands instead of catching it on your body.
3. Counter quickly and effectively until your attacker is defeated.

1. Drawing a knife:
2. When an opponent has his knife out and is threatening:
3. Attack first with kicks.
4. As this example shows, you can also shift back out of range and use side kicks.
5. Aim for the knee to disable the attacker so that he can't move around.
6, 7. Follow up.

Defense Against Multiple Attacks

We have included illustrations of some of the more common ways two or more men could attack you. Even for the experts, defending against more than one opponent is difficult. However, it can be done. When forced to defend yourself against a group, the following techniques will give you an advantage.

You must be very forceful with your counters and stay in continuous motion. Keep moving, kicking and hitting, thus making it more difficult for attackers to hit you. Being passive or standing still gives them the advantage. When possible, try to take out the strongest-appearing one of the group. Eliminate the leader first if you can. Using one of the physically weaker ones as your shield is sometimes useful. Grab a weaker attacker and try to throw him into the others as a blocking action. Use any kind of weapon available. Remember to use your belt. This will give you some added distance.

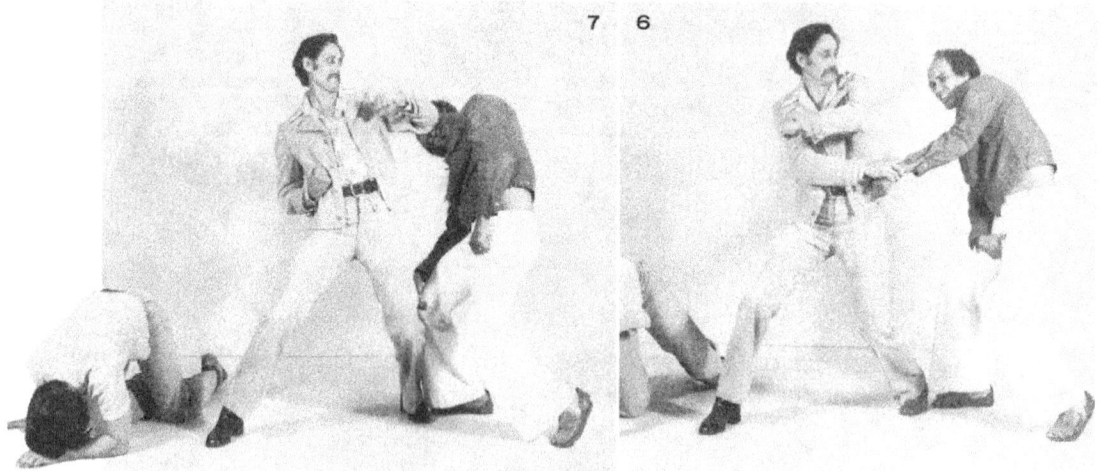

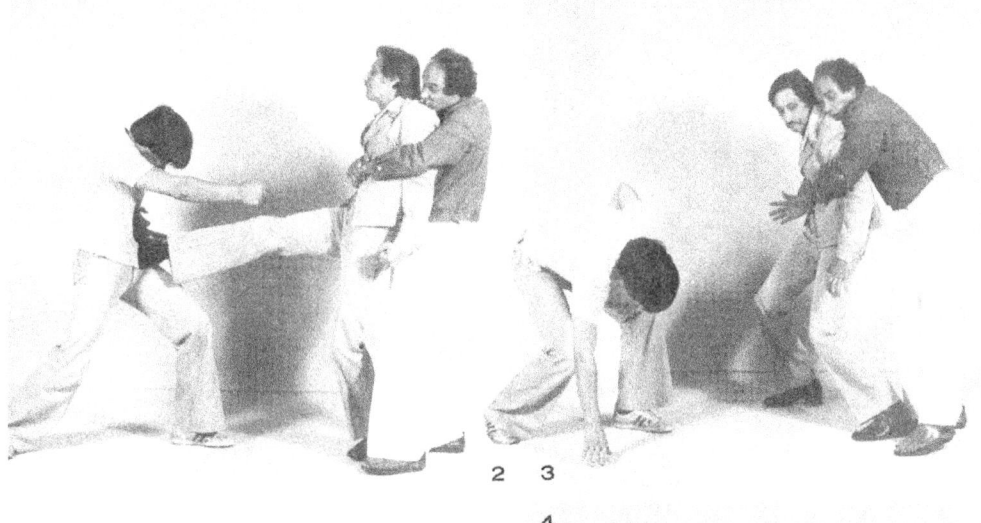

1. Two men attack:
2. Kick the man approaching you. He can cause you more harm than the one holding you.
3. Shift your weight and try to reach the groin of the one holding you. A foot stomp is also possible.
4. Continue your counterattacks back and forth to both opponents before they can recover.
5, 6, 7. Follow up.

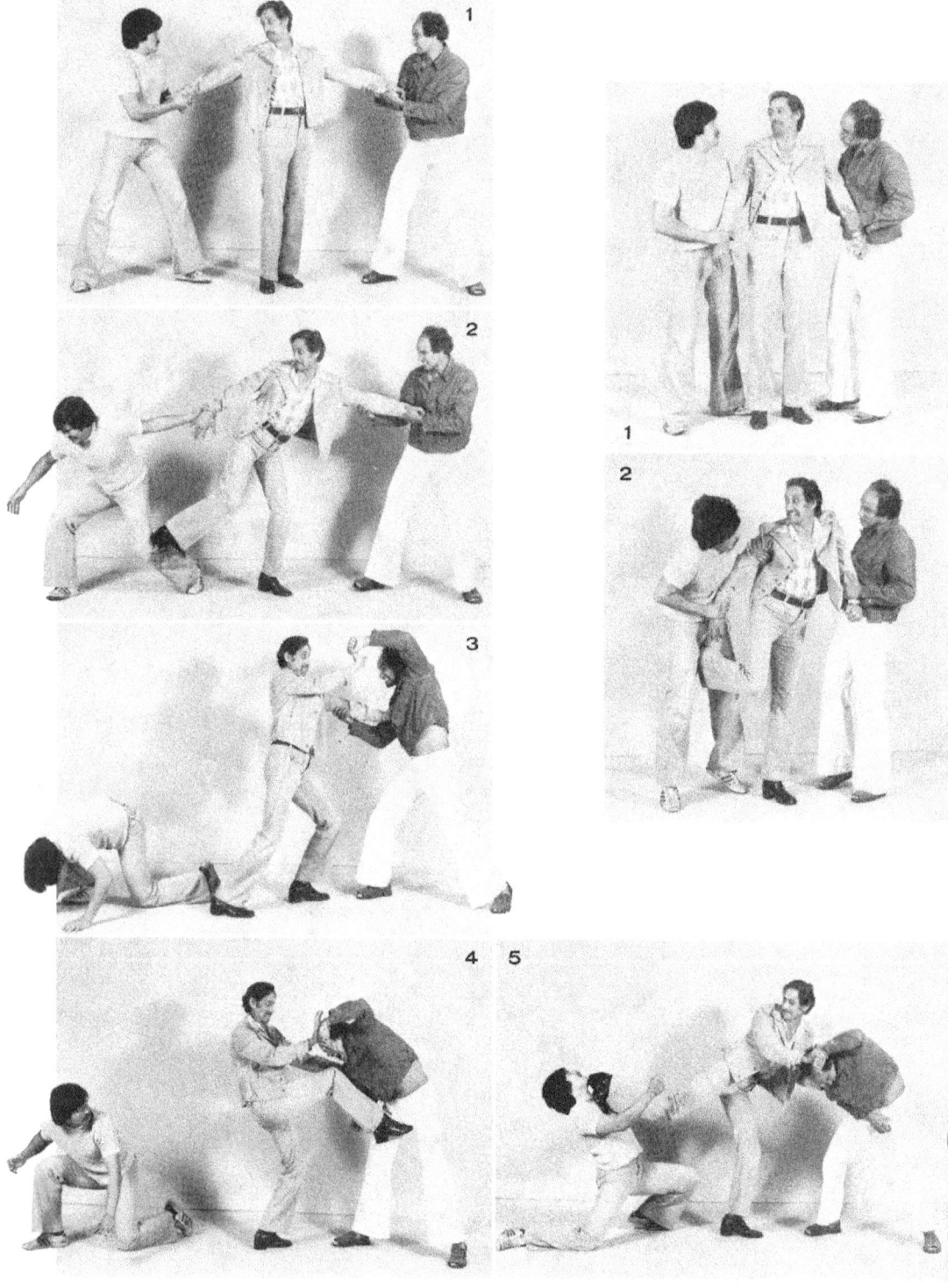

1. Two men grabbing:
2. Use your kicks. When two men are holding you tightly by the arms, you still have freedom to kick with your legs.
3. Continue kicking and striking.
4, 5. Perform the necessary follow ups.

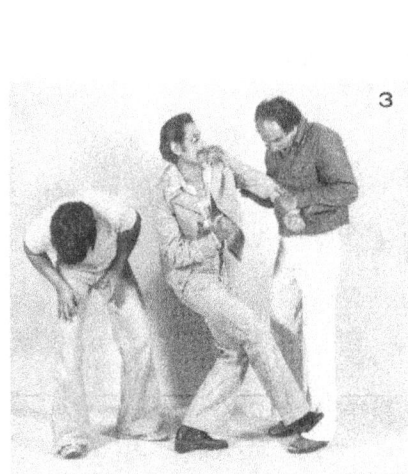

1. Two men holding:
2. Kick the one closest to you. Even with your arms outstretched you can reach attackers with your legs. Shift closer if necessary.
3. When you break free of one, concentrate your attacks on the other.
4, 5, 6, 7. Follow up with continued attacks, attending each time to the one offering the most threat.

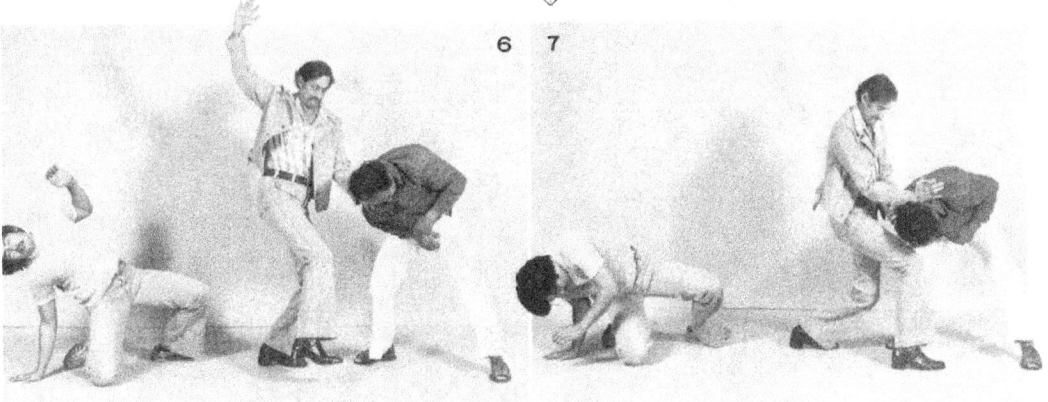

Defense Against Pistol

It must be understood from the beginning of this section that defending against an armed assailant can be fatal: any assailant that resorts to the use of a gun is to be taken seriously as mentally unstable or a hardened criminal. Both are dangerous. *WHEN DEALING WITH A GUN, DON'T VALUE MATERIAL POSSESSIONS ABOVE YOUR LIFE.* We recommend complete cooperation with an armed assailant, as do all authorities. Give him what he wants. Exception should only be made if you feel certain you will be shot or your family harmed and there is *NO OTHER RESORT.* Then we hope the following will help.

1. Pistol at body level:
2. Pivot with your arm fending off the pistol, directing the muzzle away from your body.
3. Don't allow it to point toward you while you counterattack.

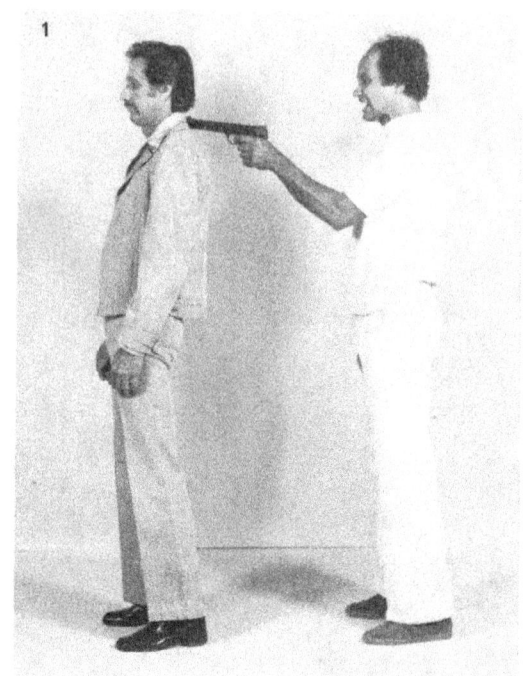

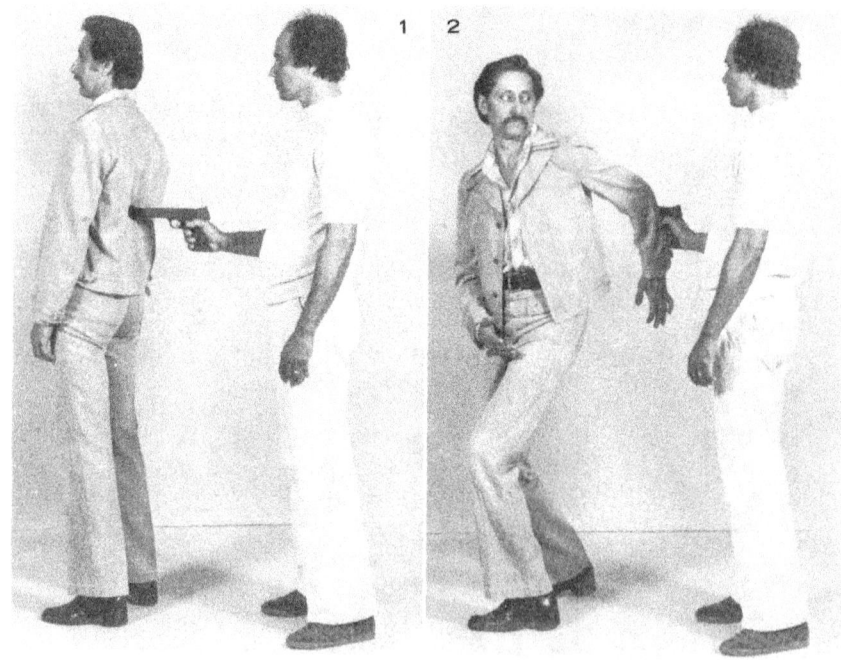

1. Pistol to your head:
2. Turn with your arm up to deflect the muzzle. In practice with blanks, students have been able to direct the path of the bullet away from their bodies before the shot goes off.
3. Counterattack quickly and repeatedly. Keep the muzzle directed away from you until your opponent is defeated.

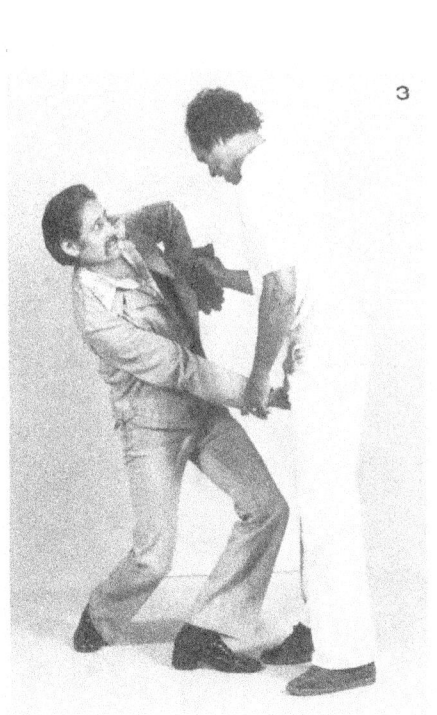

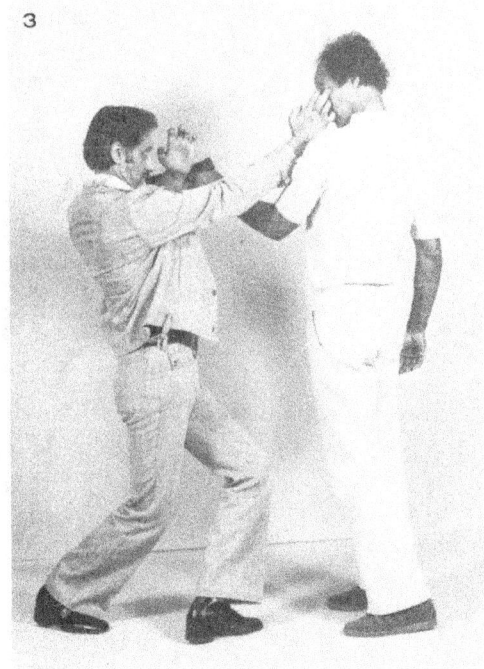

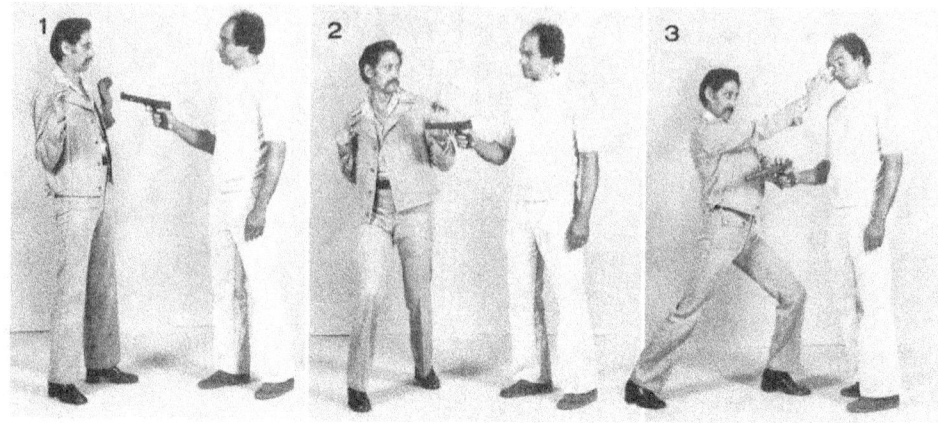

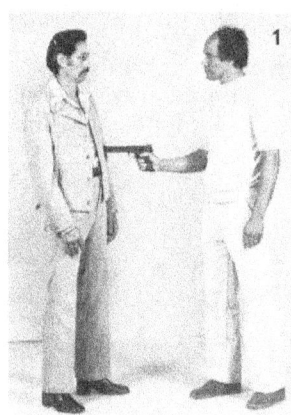

1. Facing a pistol:
2. Pivot your body and use your hands to direct the muzzle away.
3. Keep your body out of the path of the bullet, and counterattack.

1. Pistol is held lower:
2. Twist your body and use your arm to deflect.
3. Counter while directing the muzzle away from your body.

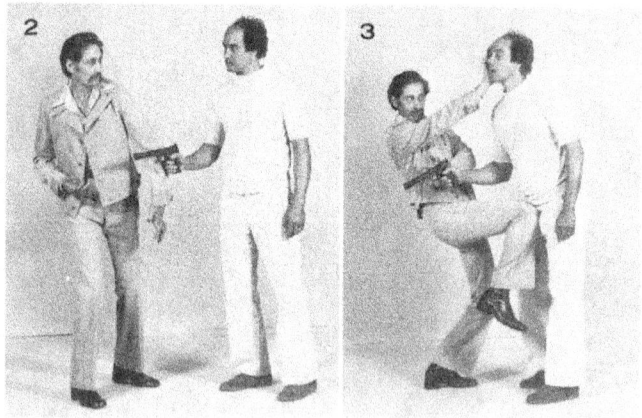

Note:
The police section will give added techniques on gun defense.

Tactics and Strategy

The following practical advice for street survival will cover situations which might have been overlooked in the series of illustrated self-defense techniques. Avoid risk areas. Another route or approach could mean more safety. Run or leave the scene as soon as you see trouble beginning. Use a weapon of any kind as an equalizer: pocket change, a comb, keys, stick or club, chair, rocks, tire iron. The list of possibilities is endless. Fight as "DIRTY" as you can. Employ biting, spitting, and gouging in addition to all other methods mentioned in this text. Use your imagination. Screaming into your opponent's face will startle him, perhaps giving you a momentary advantage. Deception is a good way to gain an advantage. Do something to distract an opponent. Offer to shake hands, for example, then kick. Some people have been able to feign heart attacks or appear ill. Get help from a friend, neighbor or passing car if possible. Attract attention any way you can. Shout and scream, throw rocks at cars and through windows, set off alarms. People sometimes ignore pleas for help so you must draw them in, involve them in some way. Fight strategically. Depending on the location of an attack choose the safest area for you. Perhaps it's out in the open with room to maneuver, or behind a table or chair, or with your back to the wall and kicking. Attack first if you see that a fight is unavoidable. Getting in the first blow or kick will give you the edge. Follow up until your opponent is incapacitated. Talk your way out of it if you feel it is possible. Apologize if the circumstances call for it. It is better to be safe than risk injury. Use your natural talents. Many can utilize training in some sport or activity. For example, a good wrestler can leg dive an opponent, pull both legs out from under him and dump him on his back or head. Football-style blocks to the body, or head butts can also help. Handball, racketball, tennis—all help to improve your reactions. Keep in shape. A healthy body is stronger and can fight harder. It's good advice to take care of your body even if you never have to use self-defense. Expect pain. Mentally prepare yourself for the possibility of getting hurt. Regardless of pain, continue to fight. Men with serious knife wounds have fought back. You too can SURVIVE.

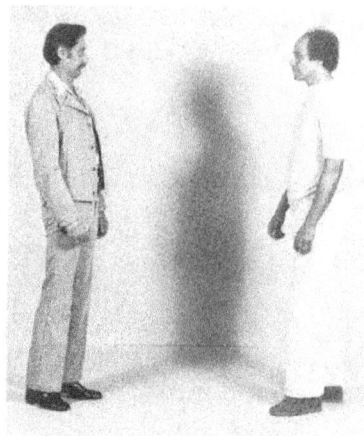

Defensive Postures

Positions:
A. Stand out of arm's reach when arguing. This gives you time to safely react in the event of a surprise attack.
B. Standing with hands crossed at your groin is an added safety precaution against a surprise kick.
C. Holding your lapel will keep your hand nearer your face for blocking or hitting.

Defensive Sparring

These are some of the positions you can assume when fighting. Keeping the back straight will help you maintain balance. Keep your hands positioned so that you can block high or low blows. Your forward hand is probably best for blocking high blows, rear hand held to block kicks. Your most extended hand can jab toward your opponent's face, with open fingers or a fist. Practice shifting, or shuffling around the room, shadow boxing to experience the feeling. Change positions frequently, maneuvering back and forth and from side to side. Keep your knees bent slightly in a crouch, legs not too far apart. Practice raising your back leg or front leg and kicking without too much "telegraphing." Always get your leg in and out again quickly, and back on the ground for good balance. Study the Karate chapter to improve your kicks.

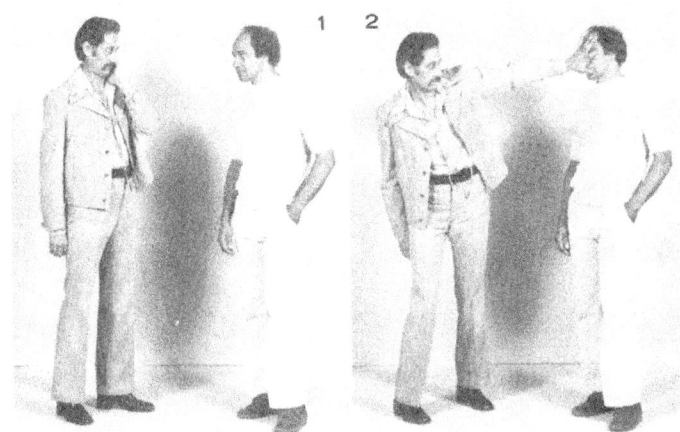

1. Scratch or rub your face or neck.
2. This offers a chance to initiate a surprise attack of your own.

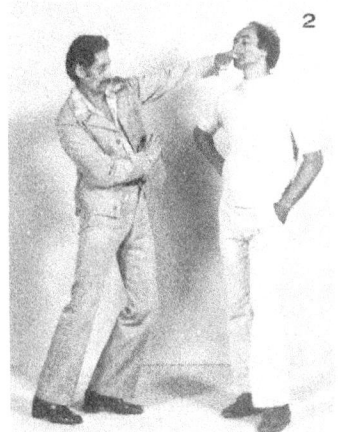

1. *Crossed arms* provide added protection. You can block low or high blows.
2. A blow to your opponent's face is unexpected from this position.

Sitting Defense

1. From a sitting position, brace yourself and kick if approached from the front.

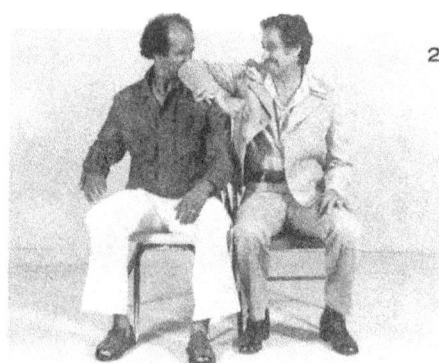

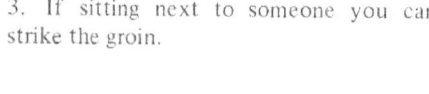

2. Use an elbow smash to the face for an attacker sitting beside you.

3. If sitting next to someone you can strike the groin.

4. Step on the attacker's foot if he is sitting beside you.

Unusual Situations

Coming at you from an auto:
1. As the aggressor is partway out of his car smash the door against him with your foot.
2. *Use your arms* to pin attacker with the car door as he is getting out.

When getting out of an auto wait until the attacker is next to your door and then smash him by pushing hard with both hands. Keep your knees braced.

Top:
When bent over hood of car (or table) use your knees and claw at his face to back him off. Follow up as soon as you can get up.

Someone following you outside: If you are in front, swing or smash the door into him. If he is in front of you, try the same thing. Take advantage of the swinging door.

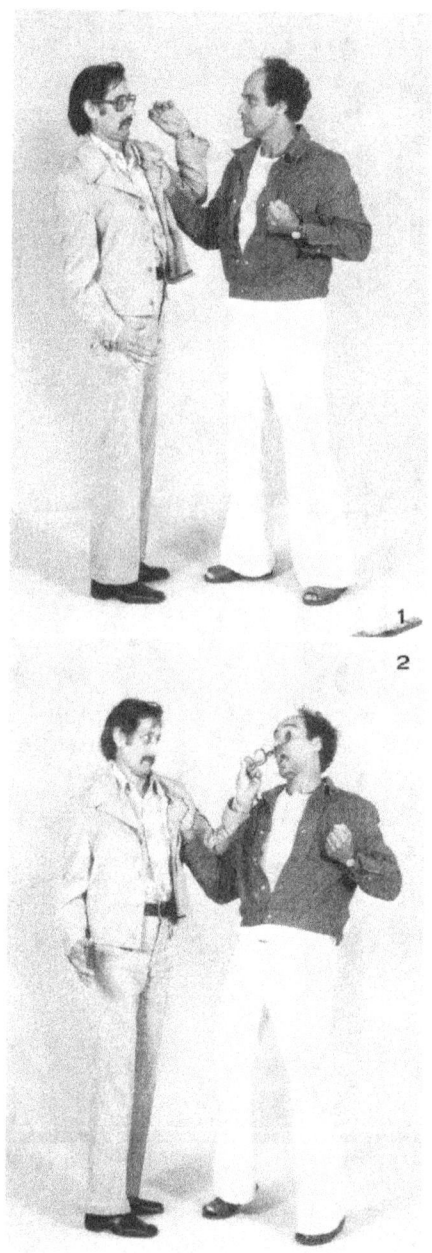

Top: ↑
Remove your glasses and thrust them into your opponent's eyes.

Using a Weapon for Defense

↑
Hit your opponent in the face with whatever you have in your hand.

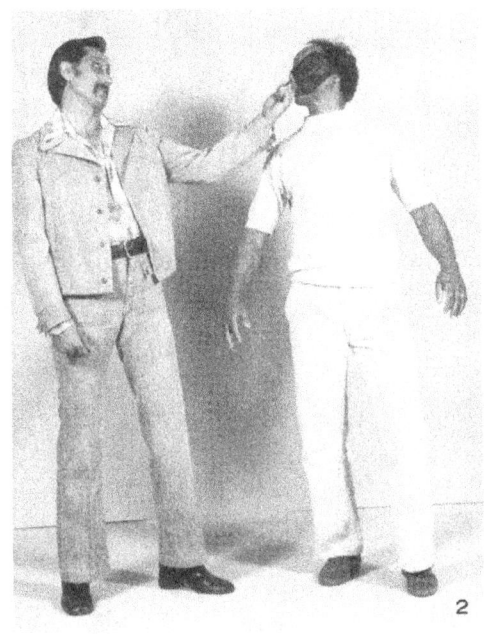

Bottom:
A rolled-up newspaper or magazine can be effective against vital targets.

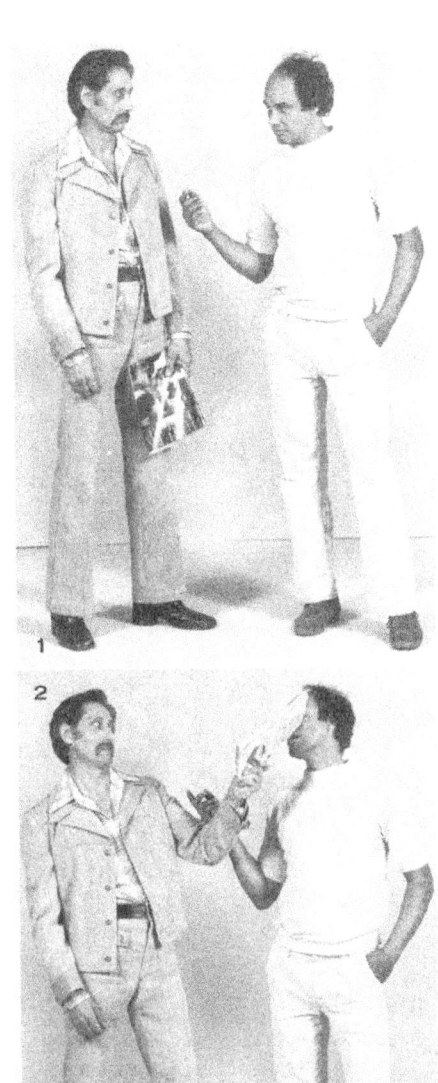

Top:
A magazine can be used. Use the stiff edge against his eyes or throat.

A broom or stick of some kind is one of the most commonly available "weapons." Thrusting with the end or overhand to the head are good blows. Swinging it like a bat is an effective maneuver.

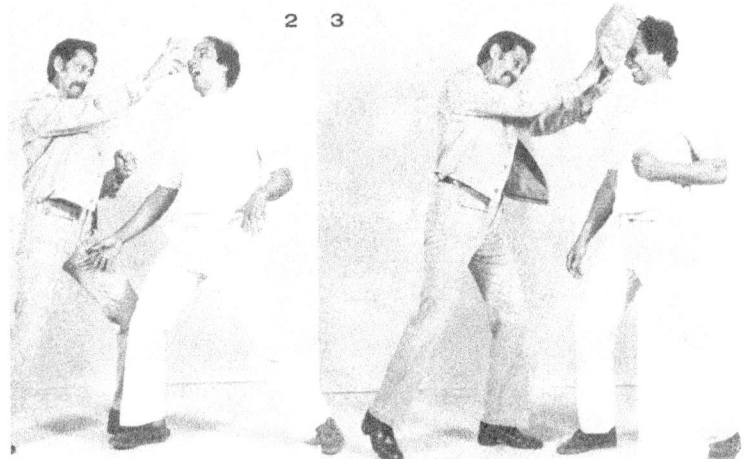

1. Keys are effective against the eyes or throat.
2. A stone, rock or brick can be thrown or used in hitting.
3. A bag or even groceries can give you an advantage.
4. Your briefcase can be thrust or swung at an opponent.
5. A length of stick is an added safety measure.

A Closer Look at Your 'Body Weapons' and How to Use Them

Groin attacks will cause the strongest men in the world to collapse. Although crude, it is very effective to squeeze and beat the groin until submission.

Dangerous blows:
In emergency situations, when you are governed by instinct and reaction, you cannot remember 'vital targets' as such. However, you can remember that extremely critical blows to use are to the throat, neck, temple, nose driven upward, groin, eyes. Throat, neck and temple blows can be fatal.

Choke right with your forearm across your opponent's windpipe. Use your other hand to form a 'vise' and tighten. (This is extremely dangerous—a ruptured windpipe can cause serious injury or death.)

The proper form for punching is to brace your legs and deliver the punch by applying your body weight behind it. The middle photo shows a 'hammer' blow, striking with the bottom fleshy part of the fist. The right photo shows an example of the backhand fist strike, used to hit someone approaching from the side.

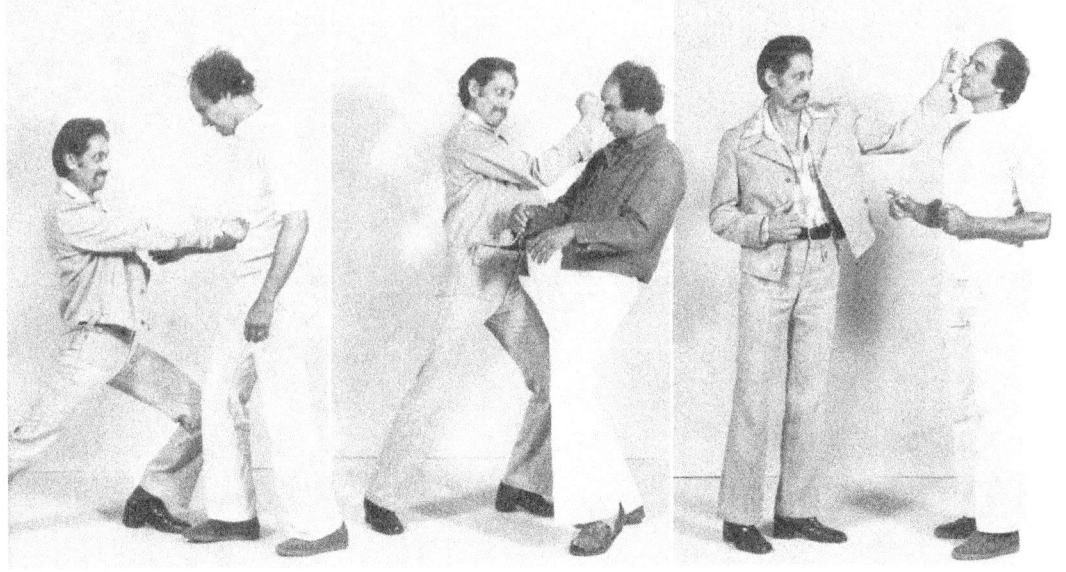

Kicking:
Most people have more power in their legs than in their arms. The legs are longer and can be used with greater safety. Illustrations are self-explanatory. Kicks to low targets are very effective and difficult to block. A low kick has more power; the higher it goes, the less power it has. For street self-defense, perform kicks low and strong.

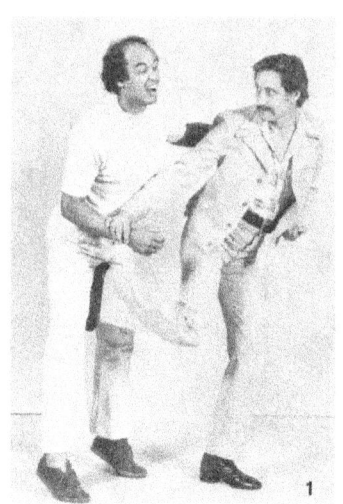

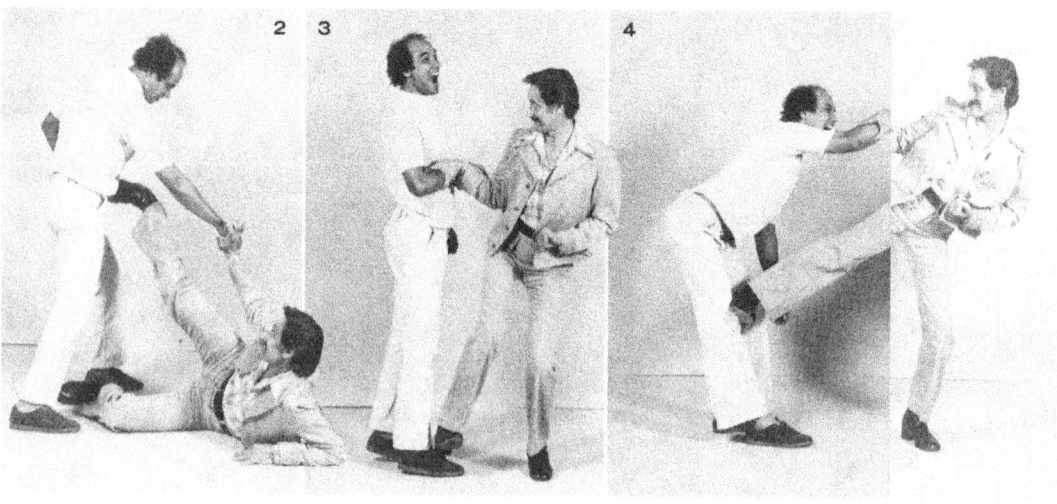

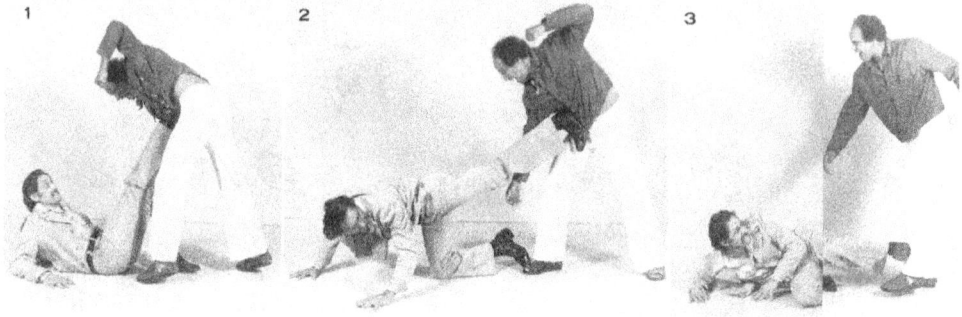

Close-up views—how to hit and where:
Use the edge of the hands to chop vulnerable areas such as the throat and neck. This procedure is very dangerous.

Use the fingertips to attack the eyes.

Your palm heel can be thrust upward, into the nose or chin.

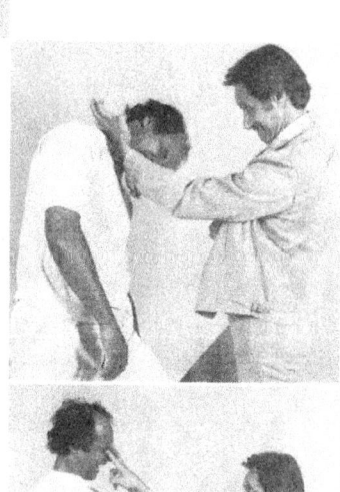

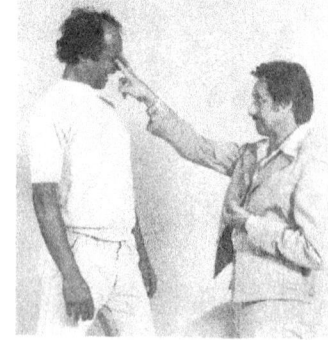

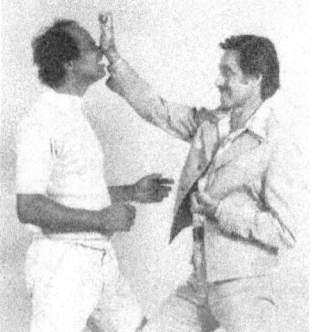

Kicking from the ground:
Stay on your feet and fight, as it's safer. However, should you be approached while sitting or lying down, or slip and fall while fighting, the following illustrations show examples of kicks to use.
1. *On your back* kicking up;
2. *Face down, kicking* with back kick;
3. *On your side* going for the shins;
4. *Tripping* by sweeping or kicking opponent's legs out from under him.

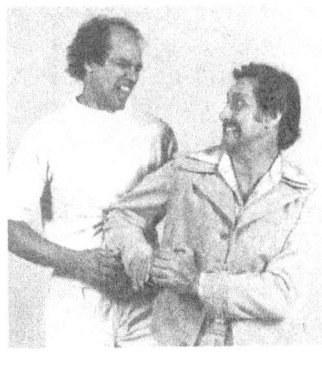

Fortify your elbow for a blow to the solar plexus. Elbow strikes are powerful and can be used from all angles when fighting at close quarters.

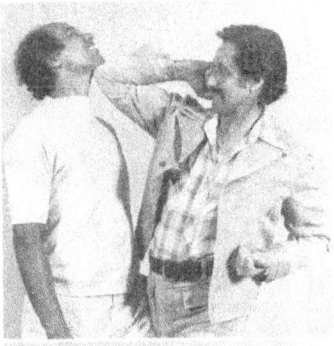

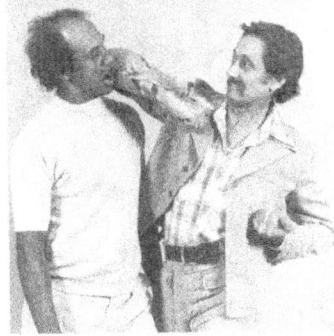

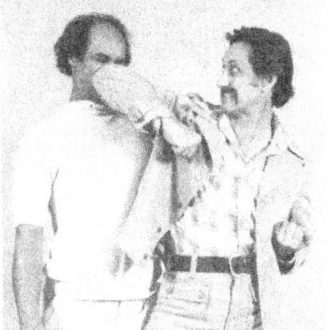

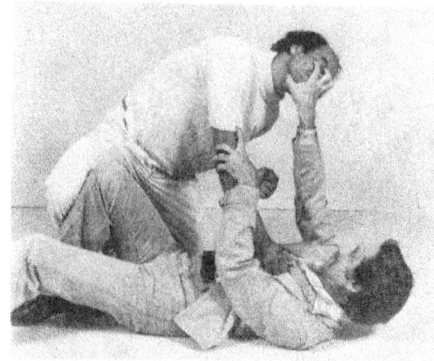

Fighting from the ground:
When grappling on the ground with an attacker, kicking and punching become more difficult. You may still do much damage by groping, gouging, ripping and tearing at the vital and sensitive targets with your fingers and hands.

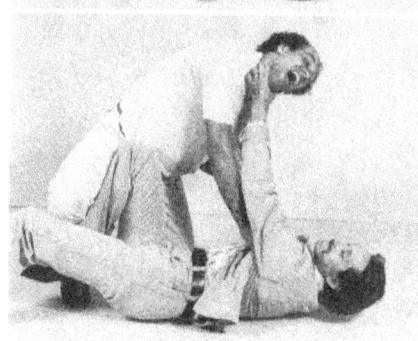

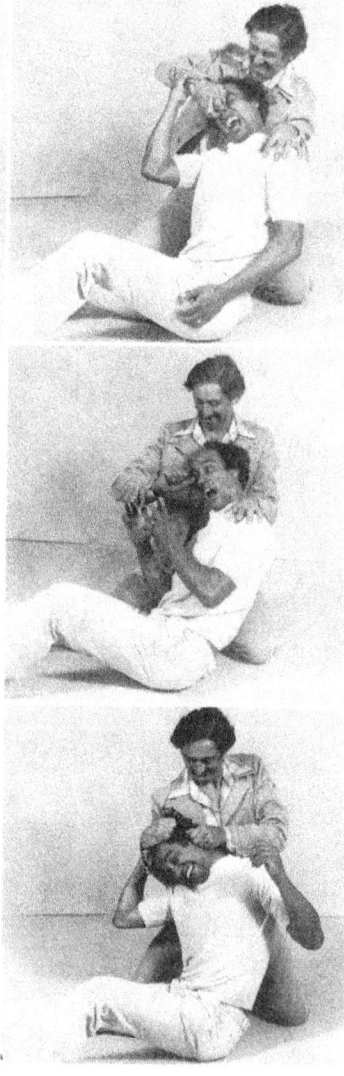

Apprehension Restraint

We wish to thank Detective Sgt. Cloyd Potter, 19-year veteran of police work, for his contribution on apprehension and restraints. Sgt. Potter has trained in Karate for the past 15 years and is a senior black belt member of the Japan Karate Federation of America. Among his many other commendable accomplishments, Sgt. Potter is a S.W.A.T. team leader for his Department as well as Weaponless Defense Instructor. In his capacity as Self-Defense Instructor, he trains not only his own department, but other police agencies and the military. Recently he has become involved in training police agencies outside the United States. Sgt. Potter has contributed a synopsis of the techniques he teaches at the above agencies. These techniques can be applied to restrain and subdue an opponent instead of resorting to the more drastic measures we have presented elsewhere. The average man in the street is interested only in protecting himself, unlike those who, by the very nature of their professions, must subdue or restrain an opponent. Chapters on Aiki-do and Judo also deal with subduing one's opponent without too much injury.

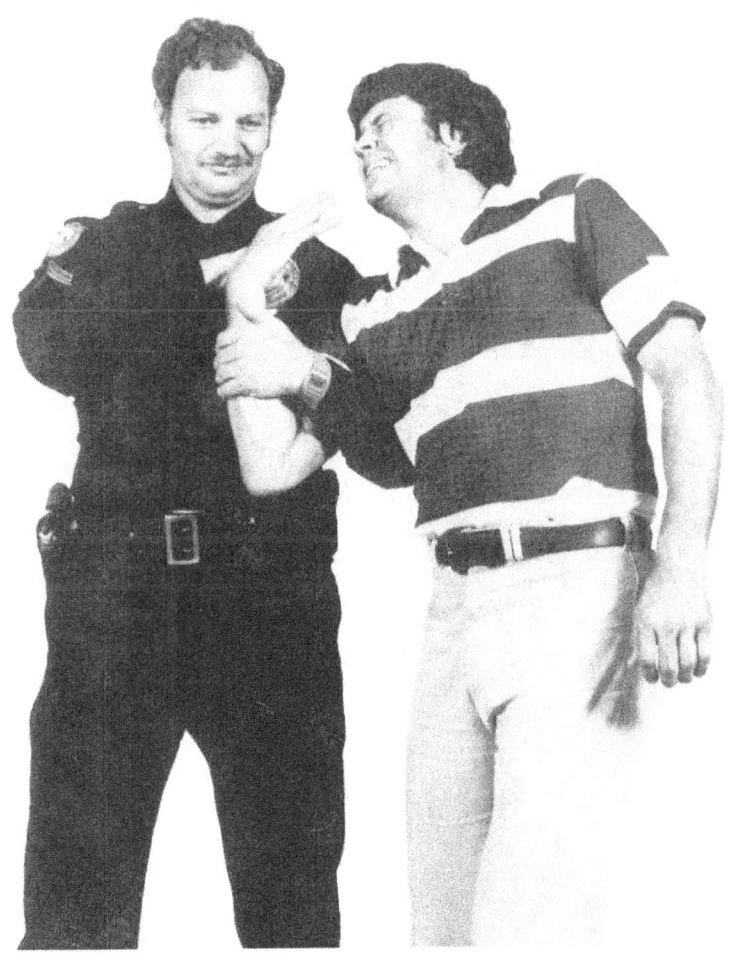

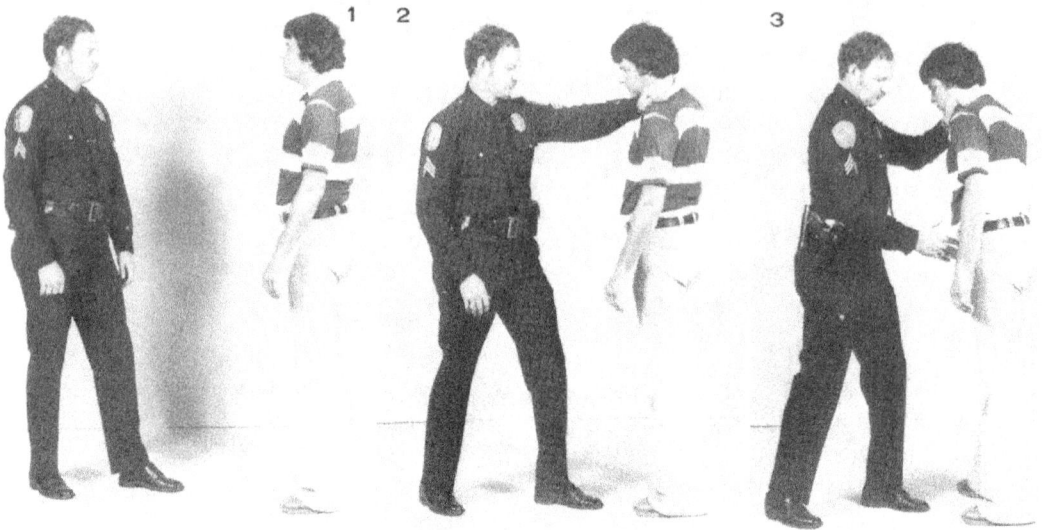

Police Apprehension

1. Arm bar take-down:
2. Grab or jolt subject by the shoulder to upset his balance.
3. Stepping in, one hand grasps at the wrist.
4. Pulling down on the shoulder, brace his arm as shown.
5, 6. Continue to force the arm upward with leverage and position yourself around to come up beside or behind him.
7. This is the leverage position you want to attain. Practice getting to this point. Hands are clasped and your forearm is applying pressure to his arm.
8, 9. Drop to the ground, forcing him ahead of you face down. Kneel, staying well-balanced and in control. Now, handcuffs can be applied.

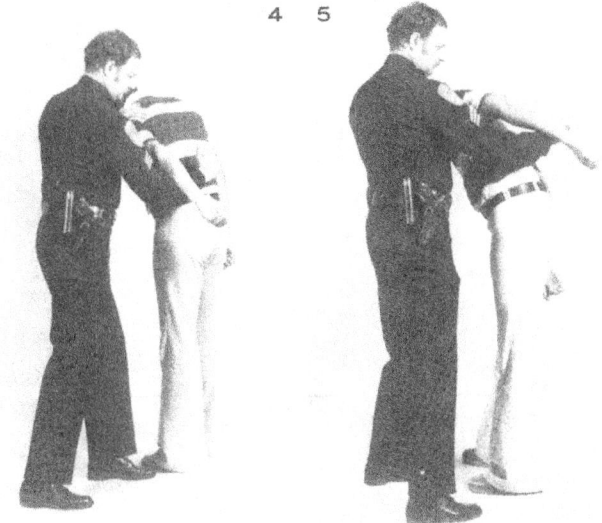

Note:
Officers consider this one of the most oft-used and reliable techniques. It is safest to bring subject face down as he cannot kick or strike back easily.

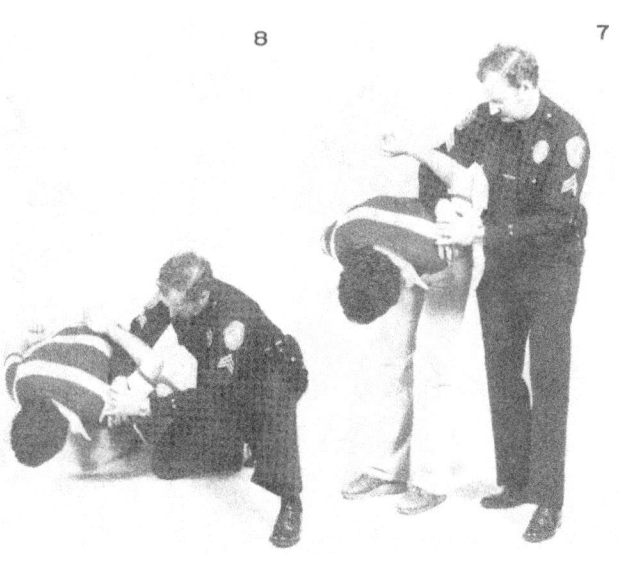

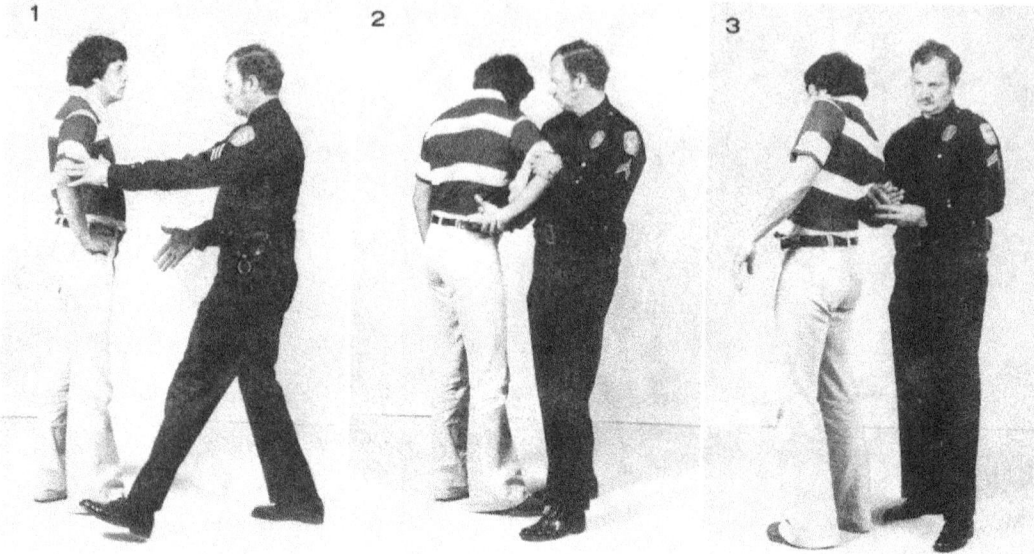

1. Hammer lock take-down:
2. Taking opponent's arm with one hand, grasp his hand with your other hand. Step in and to the side.
3. Cradle his elbow in your arm and pull his hand back as shown, applying pressure against the hand and wrist and up against the elbow and shoulder.

4. Should it be necessary to follow up, bring him down by pulling at the shoulder and neck.
5. As he drops on to his back, flip him over. You can even bring him down to your knee and hold from there, or flip him on his stomach and still maintain pressure on the wrist.

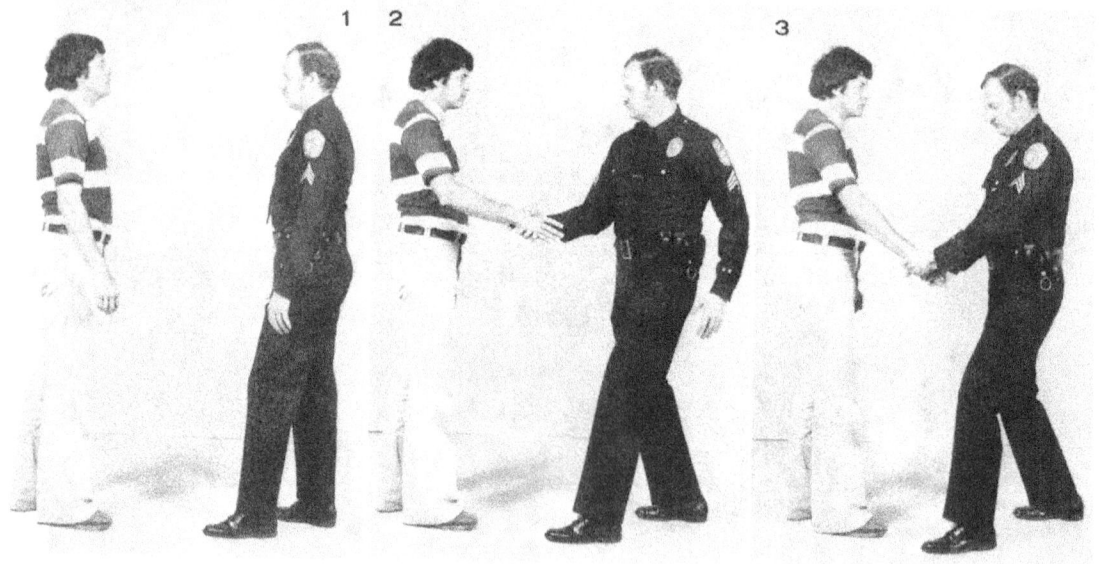

1. Take-down:
2. Offering to shake hands can distract a subject. Alternately, simply reach out and take his hand.
3. Grab firmly with both your hands. Step through and under his arm.
4. In the illustration his right leg steps in so he can come under the subject's arm as he raises it above head level. Pivot your body around to come out in the position shown.
5. Pull down sharply, applying elbow pressure.
6. Force the subject to the floor.

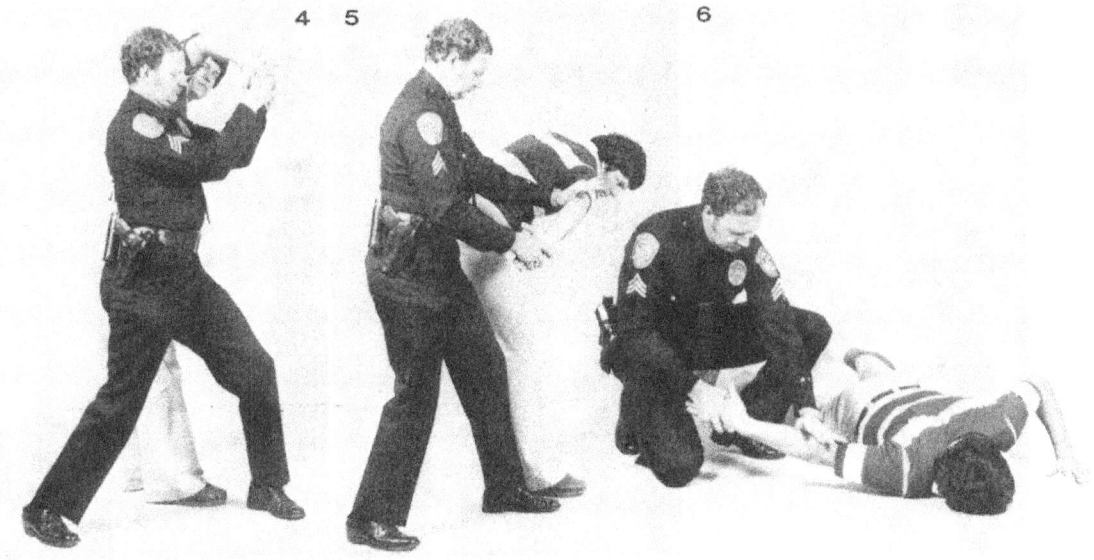

1. Thumb leverage:
2. Reach for the subject's arm as shown, one hand grabbing his elbow, the other the thumb.
3. Shift your weight and slide in close to his side. Brace his arm as shown and pull down on the thumb. This will cause extreme pain.

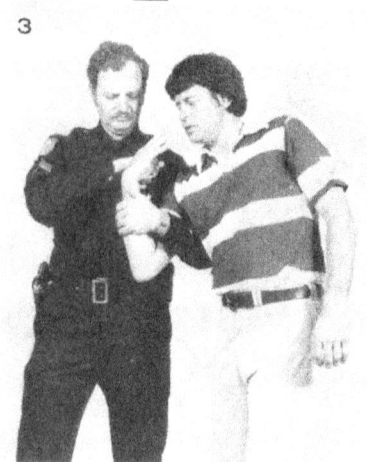

1. Wrist pressure:
2. Grasping the subject's arm and hand as shown, step in and to the side.
3. Cradle his arm securely as shown.
4. By applying pressure to his wrist with both of your hands, you will cause extreme pain. Subject can be brought to the ground from this position by merely pulling down and forward quickly.

1. Thumb leverage variation:
2. Grasp his arm and thumb as shown.
3. Continue as in the previous thumb leverage exercise except for the hand position of the subject. Practice using both methods depending on the initial grasp of subject's hand and his positions.

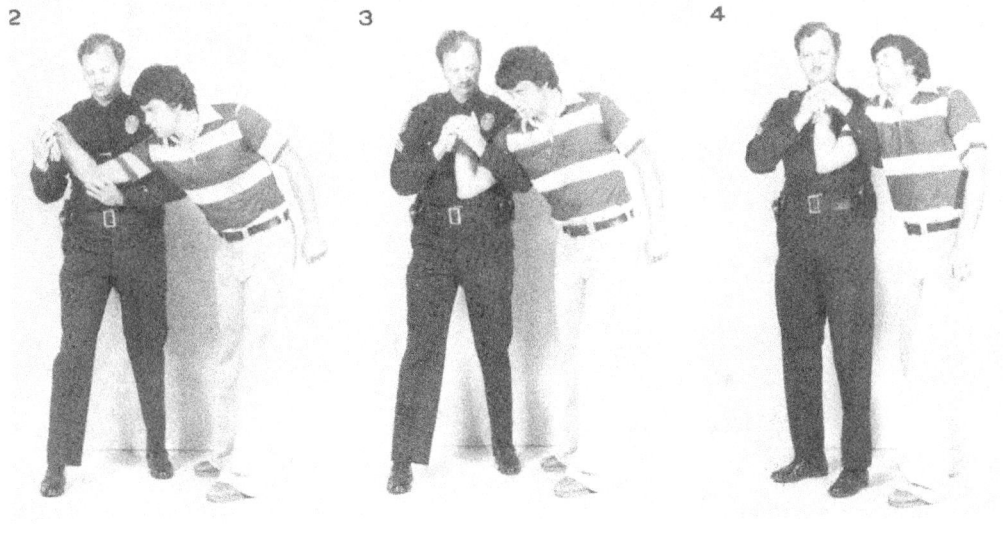

1. Leg sweep:
2. Brace your leg behind the subject as shown.
Note:
To bring subject down, raise your leg in a sweeping action, in effect kicking his leg out from under him. When practicing, be sure you step in deep enough and don't get off balance. Lean your shoulder into him to move his center of gravity back.

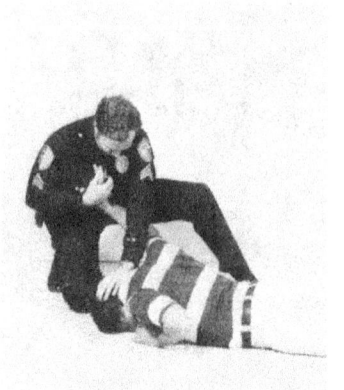

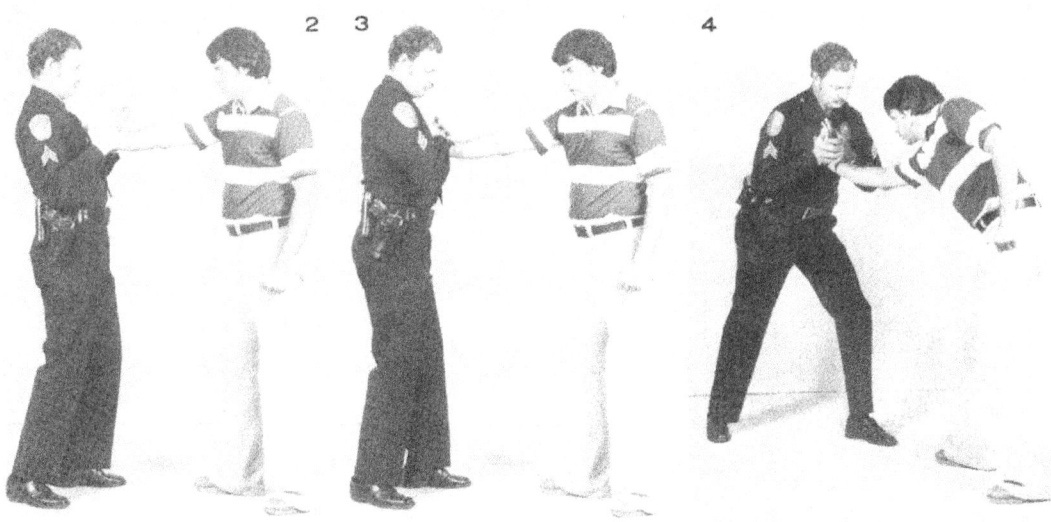

1. Pushing:
2. When the subject pushes you;
3. Clasp both of your hands over his, holding it tightly to your chest.
4, 5, 6. Pull your legs back and go into a kneeling position, keeping pressure against his hand and wrist.
7, 8. When low enough, grasp his head and pull him to the ground.

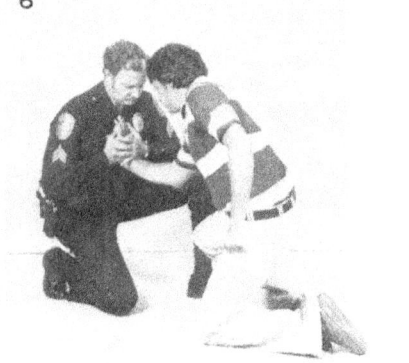

1. Punching:
2. Defend with your forearm blocking the punch. Shift your body to the outside of the punch.
3, 4. Pivot toward him and grab his extended arm, as shown.
5, 6, 7. Pressure applied against the elbow will force him down.
8. Subject can be taken to the ground on his stomach.

5

6

7

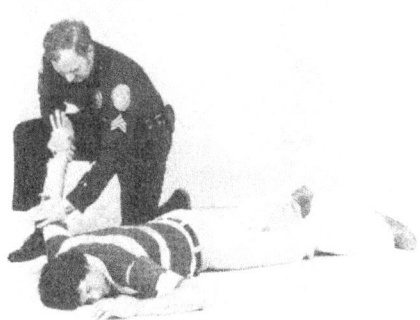
8

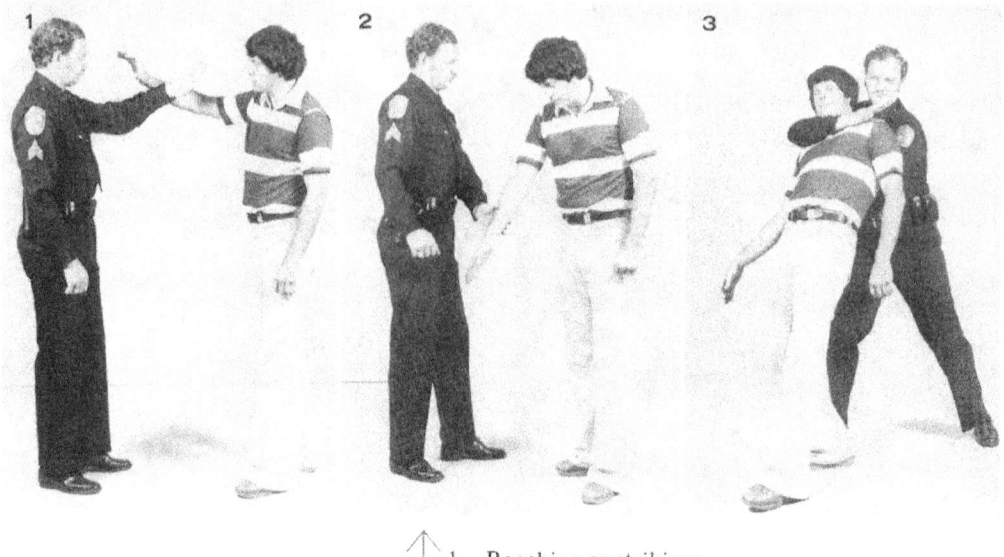

1. Reaching or striking:
2. Block with your hand as shown. Throw his arm in a circle. You can, with practice, effectively throw your subject off balance by swinging his arm sharply in a large circle across his own body.
3. Step around behind him while he is off balance and bring your arm in position across his neck.
4. This illustration shows your arm across his back, braced.
5. As you pull him down, reach for his hand. Brace on your knee.
6. Holding his hand, use it to flip him over on his stomach and place your knee on his back.

1. Outside wrist take-down:
2. Grab your opponent's extended hand with both your hands.
3. Hold with your thumbs on the back of his hand, your fingertips in his palm.
4. Twist sharply to the outside, dropping him to his back.
5. To get him on his stomach pull up on his arm and use it to pull him over.
6. Additional wrist pressure can be applied as shown.

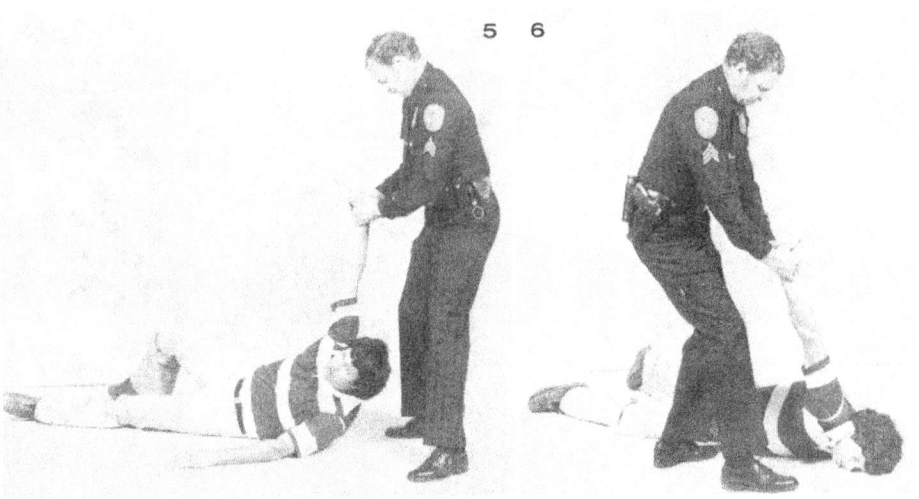

1. Facing a pistol:
2. Pivot your body out of the path of the bullet and grasp for the barrel. Your hand moves faster than your body so grab and deflect first as you move.
3, 4, 5. Keep the barrel or muzzle pointed away from your body.
6. Note the leverage used to point the barrel at the subject, and tearing it from his grasp. Your knees and kicks could justifyably be used under these conditions.

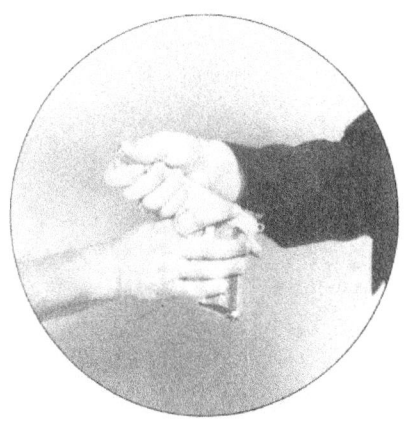

Disarming subject with a gun:
In the Self-Defense section, the subject of disarming someone with a gun was covered quite adequately. Sgt. Potter agrees with other authorities in cautioning that it should be a matter of life or death before the average man tackles a gun. The policeman must use his own judgment. Conditions and circumstances, his duty as an officer assigned to protect the community, will all be important factors that dictate the action he must take. Here then, are techniques for disarming an assailant with a gun.

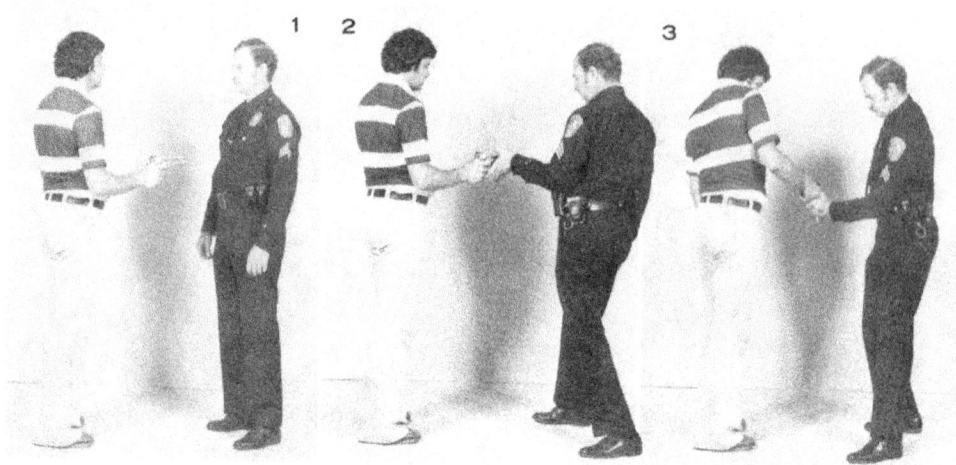

1. Facing a pistol:
2. Deflect it to the side as shown.
3. Grabbing the barrel, point it downward. A stray shot could harm innocent bystanders, therefore get the muzzle of the barrel pointed downward where it can do less harm.
4, 5, 6. The illustrations show the use of leverage to pry the gun from subject's hand. Keep in mind that while the hands are occupied deflecting the gun, you can knee your opponent in the groin.

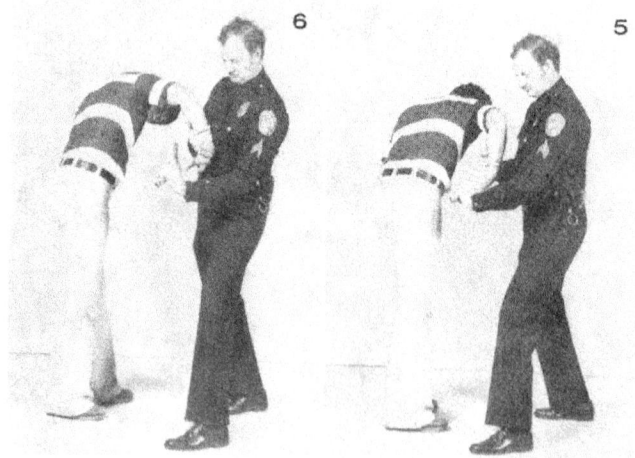

Karate

Of all the martial arts to come to us from the Far East, Karate, with Kung-fu and Tae-Kwon-do, has probably enjoyed the fastest growth in the West. The term Karate is Japanese, whereas the Chinese term is Kung-fu (American pronunciation), the Koreans call their art Tae-kwon-do and so on, varying from country to country. The translation of the word Karate is KARA implying *empty*, and TE meaning *hand*. Centuries-old art and lithographs of Japan indicate that this form of combat has existed as long as they have. Only recently, during the 1900's, has Japan offered government acceptance of Karate by inviting Okinawan masters to demonstrate it to the Japanese people. Martial arts historians generally agree that China is the mother land of all combative arts, just as she is believed to be the cradle of all Asian culture. There are differences and similarities among the fighting arts such as Karate, Tae-Kwon-do, Kung-fu and even Tai kick boxing. National pride plays an important part in perpetuating the differences, but in the final analysis, one can also see the similarities. Today different uses have evolved for the Karate style fighting: sport, art form, Tai style boxing, exercise. However, these arts were practiced as methods of defense against oppressors during the formative years. According to popular belief, Karate originated with the monks and priests of China. True or not, some records indicate that they certainly had an important part in its practice. Since World War II, it has become an important part of the physical education program of almost every major university in Japan. This trend can also be found in the United States, Europe and many, many other countries throughout the world. The devasting power to break bricks, smash tile and destroy enemies has become legend in the world of Karate. In all truth, one does kick, hit, and strike with great force when practicing Karate. This is due, in fact, to the use of proper technique based on balance, leverage, concentration of power, and channelling of energy into a single move, plus endless hours of practice. This brings us to the subject of this chapter. In order to be more effective in street fighting, one must learn the fundamental principles of Karate. We have included in this section only those methods directly applicable to use in the street, and by no means all of them. Many volumes the size of this one would be required to adequately cover the subject of Karate. We have taken into consideration the fact that you are starting from a basic position as a novice, so we are not trying to make you a Karate expert, but instead, a survivor in a street fight.

Punching

To hit someone with a closed fist is the universal way of fighting. There are basic principles of delivering a punch that will give you more effectiveness when learned and applied. One is that the wild haymaker style punch so popular in the movies looks great on the screen, but is not the best way to do it. First, your punch should always travel in a straight line to the target. A circular punch, if an opponent is guarding his face, is still 'straight' to the target. Do not make any extra or unnecessary moves that might dissipate power. A twist of the arm and wrist adds somewhat to the force. Proper balance allows you to transmit power from the ground, through the legs, into the hips, and from the hips to the back, arm and fist. *THROW A LOT OF BODY INTO THE PUNCH.* This should be done without 'overpunching' or overextending so as to lose balance. The contact surface of your fist is the two foreknuckles, the first two knuckles next to the thumb, which is wrapped securely across the bottom of the fingers. Placing your fist against a wall will demonstrate that proper contact is made with only two knuckles of the fist. On the following pages we have given you some examples and exercises to practice. We have discovered, in training thousands of people, that these simple exercises will definitely add to the impact and power of your punch.

1

Proper leg position or stance: Stand with one leg back to drive the punch with a feeling of coming from the floor. Stand and rotate arms from this stance, trying to bring into play the hips. As the punch reaches its destination get the feel of driving it with your legs.

1

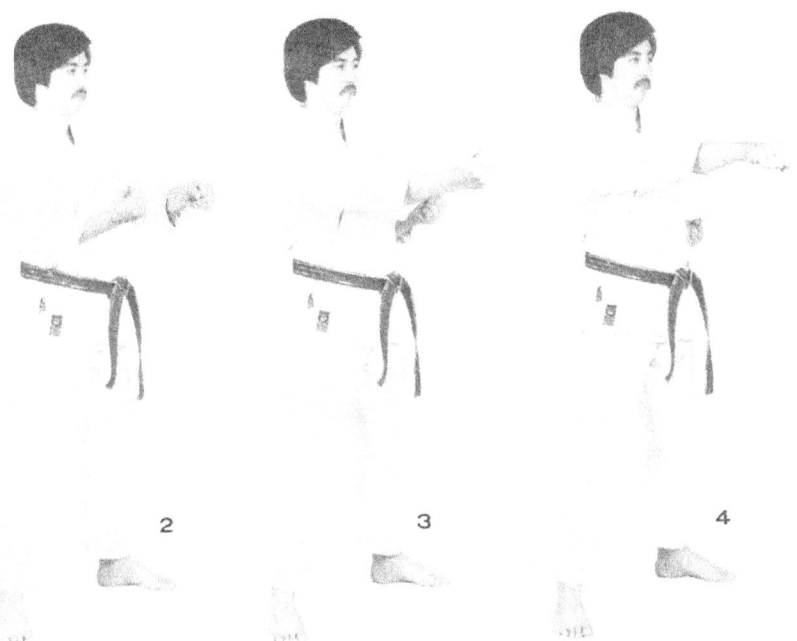

Rotating the punch: Stand still and concentrate on the rotation or twist of the punch. Thrust one hand out while sharply withdrawing the other. Start slowly and build up speed until you can actually feel the snap of the muscle as it drives into position.

Advancing with punch: Advancing on a moving target is an important step to learn. Most opponents will be shuffling about, so you must learn to catch them in order to hit them. The fundamental steps shown here will help you advance on your target with balance.
1. Starting position. Keep your back straight.
2. Step up with your back leg, closing your thighs for stronger balance.
3. Continue stepping in with forward movement.
4. Snap the punch so that it lands as your body reaches the target.

Note:

The basic position of hand on the hip is only for 'self-practice'. In actual combat, hold your hands in defense positions and go back and forth maintaining this posture.

1. Jab and punch:
2. During all maneuvering and fighting, hold your hands in the defense position.
3. Slide forward with forward leg and use forward hand in jabbing at opponent.
4. Follow up the jab with another punch with the back fist.
5, 6. Thus a simple one-two punch with a little slide to close distance between you and your opponent is completed. Keep your back straight, twist the punches and throw the body into it without over-balancing.

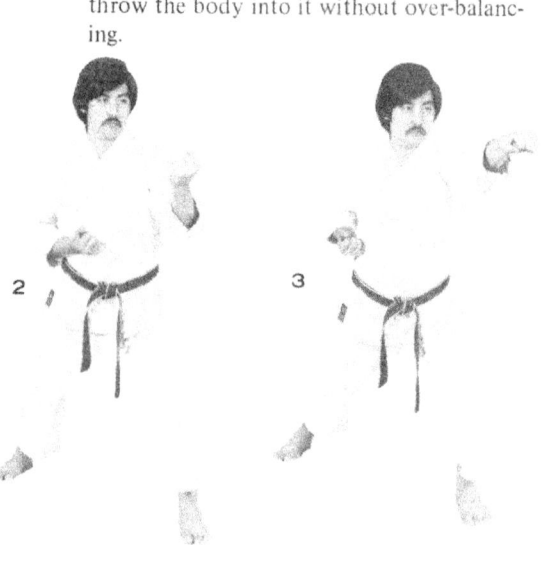

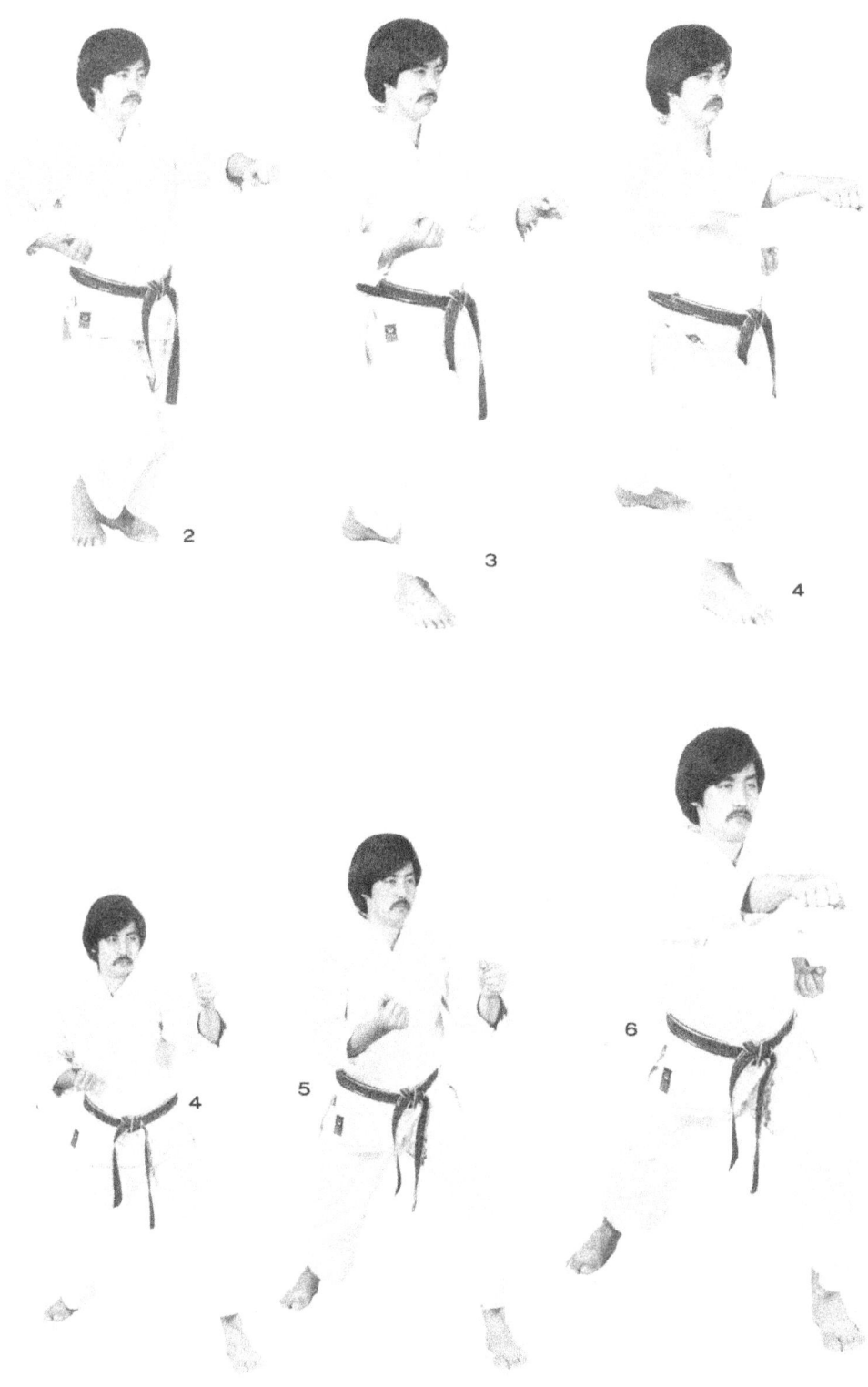

Stances

We have postponed our discussion of stances until you have attempted some actions. You will have realized by now that footwork, or stances as we will refer to it, is very critical. You must be able to shift in and out, back and forth, side to side. It takes practice to be able to do this smoothly and without jerky motions. Boxers spend hours shadowboxing. With Karate you should do the same. Imagine opponents around you and practice delivering blocks, kicks and punches in all directions. Always keep erect for better balance and don't leave yourself open. Keep your guard up, and strive for proper distance from the target —getting back out of range when attacked and closing in for the counter-attack.

1. Forward stance: Front view and side view. Allows you to have maximum driving power. You can brace against strong front attacks. Your weight is on your front leg.

2. Back stance: Front view and side view. Good defensive stance, with most of your weight on your back leg. Front leg can kick.

3. Cat stance: Front view and side view. Your weight is mostly on your back leg. Front leg free to kick. Very maneuverable stance useful in defense and offense.

4. Side stance: When attacked from the side, this stance allows you to drop away from the attack and brace yourself. Primarily for defensive use, but can be used for hand counters.

Note:

Stances are inter changeable. Be able to go from one to the other smoothly and without awkwardness. Stay loose and flexible when moving about freely, assuming a stance only long enough to apply a technique and then quickly moving on to the next best position. Example: if attacked, you may block using a back stance, but then counter going into your forward stance, and even follow that by going into the Cat stance to keep the attacker off with your front kick. Imitate a tiger watching his prey, wait for an opening, then pounce on it. With your back straight, crouch or duck from attacks, then stand erect again and keep moving. A moving target is harder to hit than a still one.

Karate Strikes

1. Open fingers: Attack the eyes and throat. Offers added length.
2. Palm heel: Drive up into chin, face, nose.
3, 4. Elbow strikes: These positions were covered in the self-defense section.
5. Claw: Good for gouging and raking face, groin, eyes.
6. Two-finger prong: Eye attacks.
7. Finger thrust: Like a spear to the solar plexus.
8. Knuckle: Extend knuckle to hit at eye, throat, solar plexus, etc.

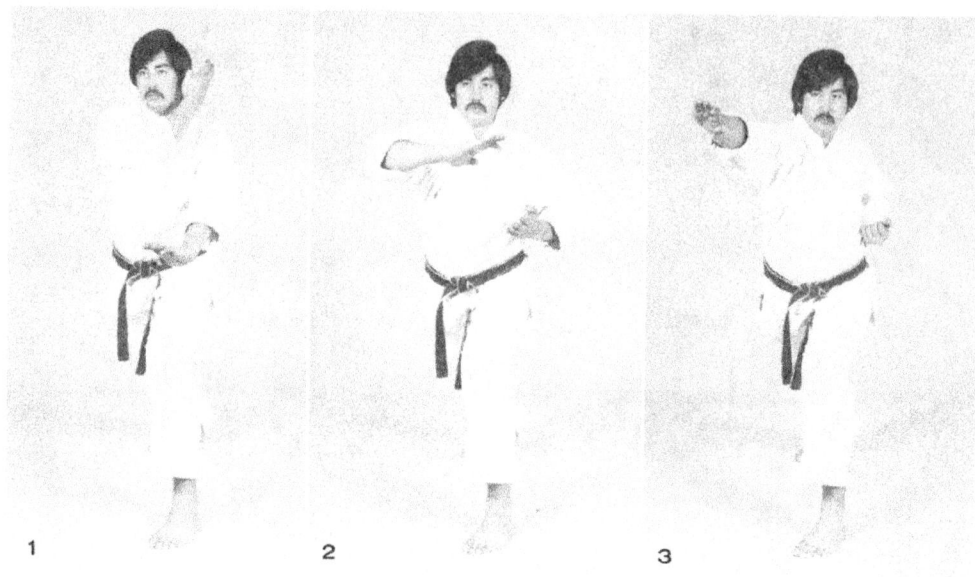

Chop: Top sequence illustrates the backhand swing and chop. Contact is made with ridge edge of hand. Bottom sequence illustrates the circular chop, snapping sharply into target area. Apply the same principles as are used in punching, concentrating your entire body muscle from the ground up, into all blows.

Backhand blow:
1, 2. These photographs illustrate the beginning of a blow to opponents standing to the side of you.
3, 4. These illustrate two different ways of hitting with the backfist. You can hit into the face or body.

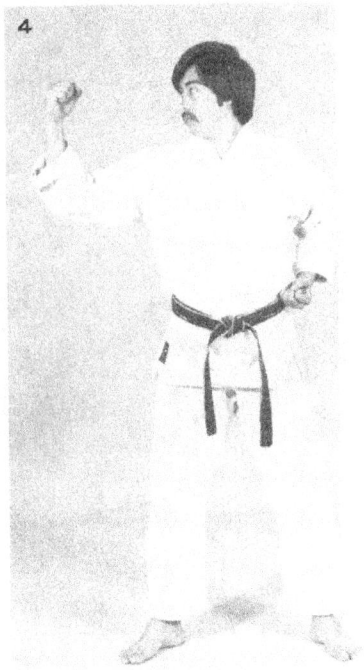

Kicking

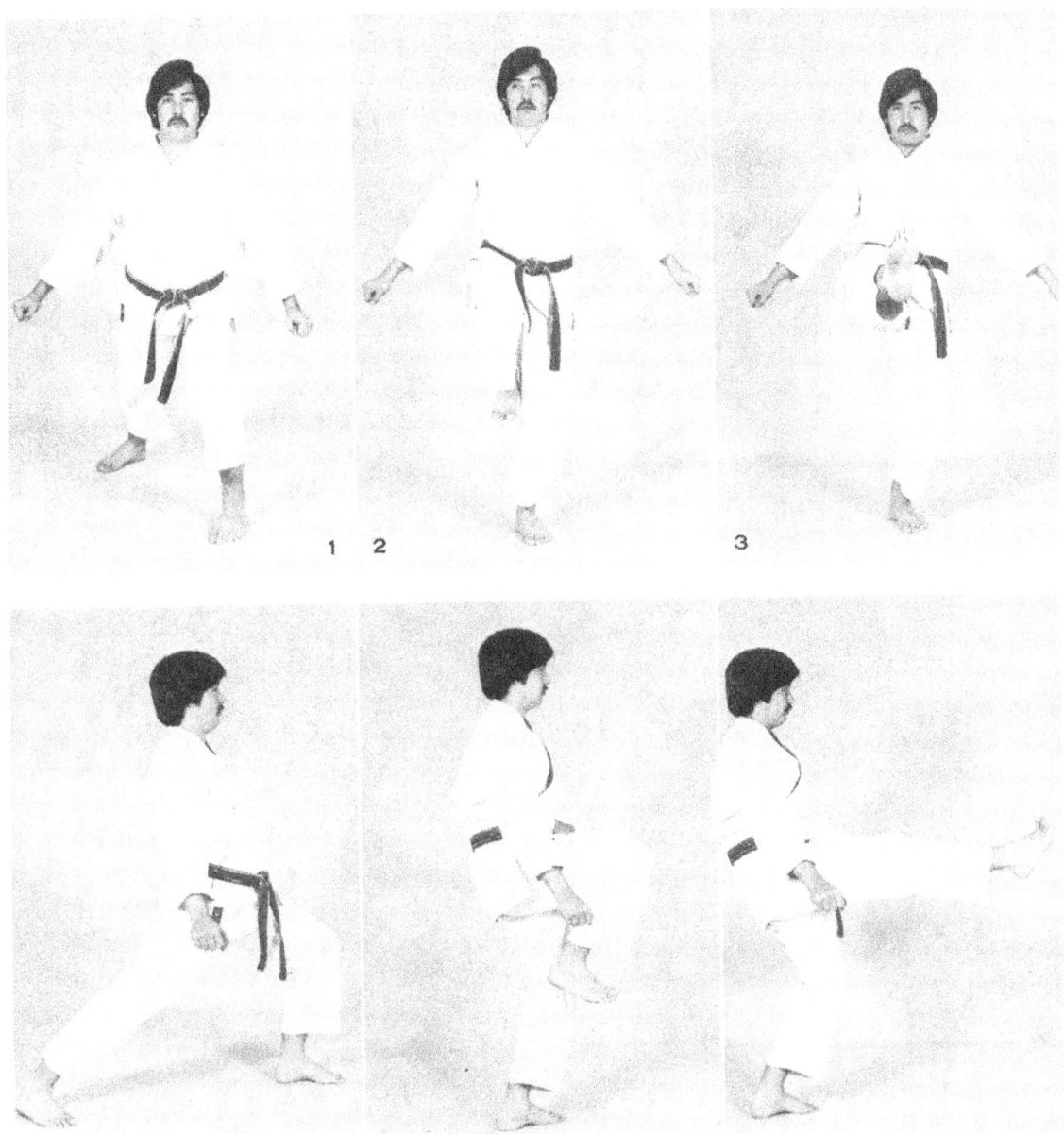

Front kick: Front and side views.
1. Basic practice stance.
2. Raise the leg to prepare the muscle.
3. Snap the leg out and back again very quickly. Hit with the toe of your shoe. This procedure is like snapping a towel or rope.

Side snap kick:
1. Prepare in this way for attacks from the side.
2. Raise leg, sole of foot turned in.
3. Snap outward, hitting with side edge of foot or shoe.
4. After contact is made snap the foot back to original position and return to floor.

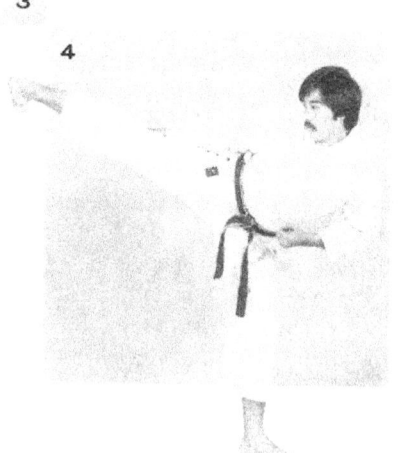

Side thrust kick:
1. The basic preparation for practice is with knees bent.
2. Raise your leg with knee forward; look to the side.

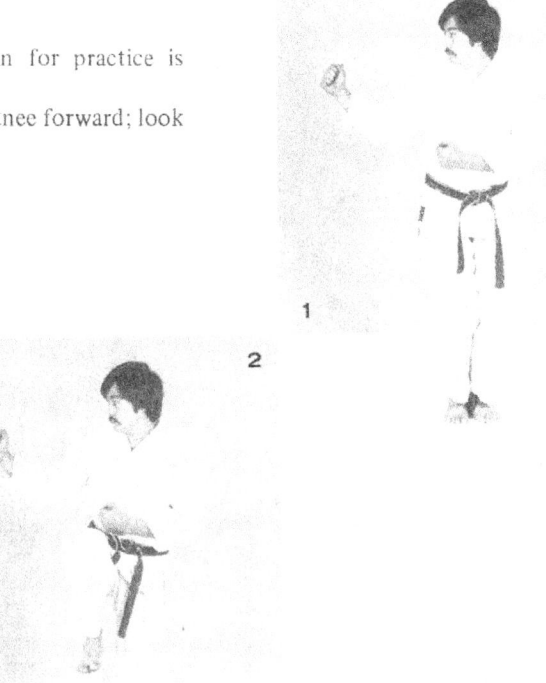

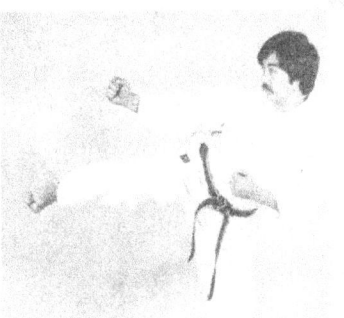

3. Thrust leg out forcefully. Make contact with the side edge of your foot or shoe.
4. Thrust all leg and buttocks muscle into this driving kick. Return it sharply to the floor, the same way it went out. This is stronger than the snap kick in that it uses more muscle drive behind it.

Roundhouse kick: This is a circular hit into the target. Raise your leg to prepare the muscle as shown. Pivot your body in the direction of the kick, snap the leg out AND BACK. Return it to the floor quickly to maintain balance.

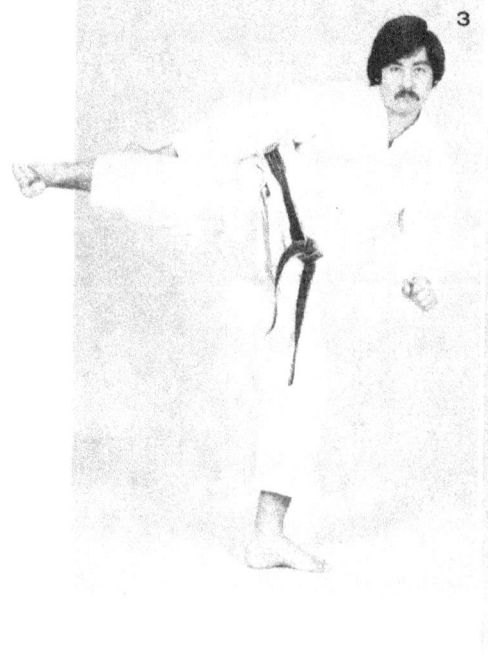

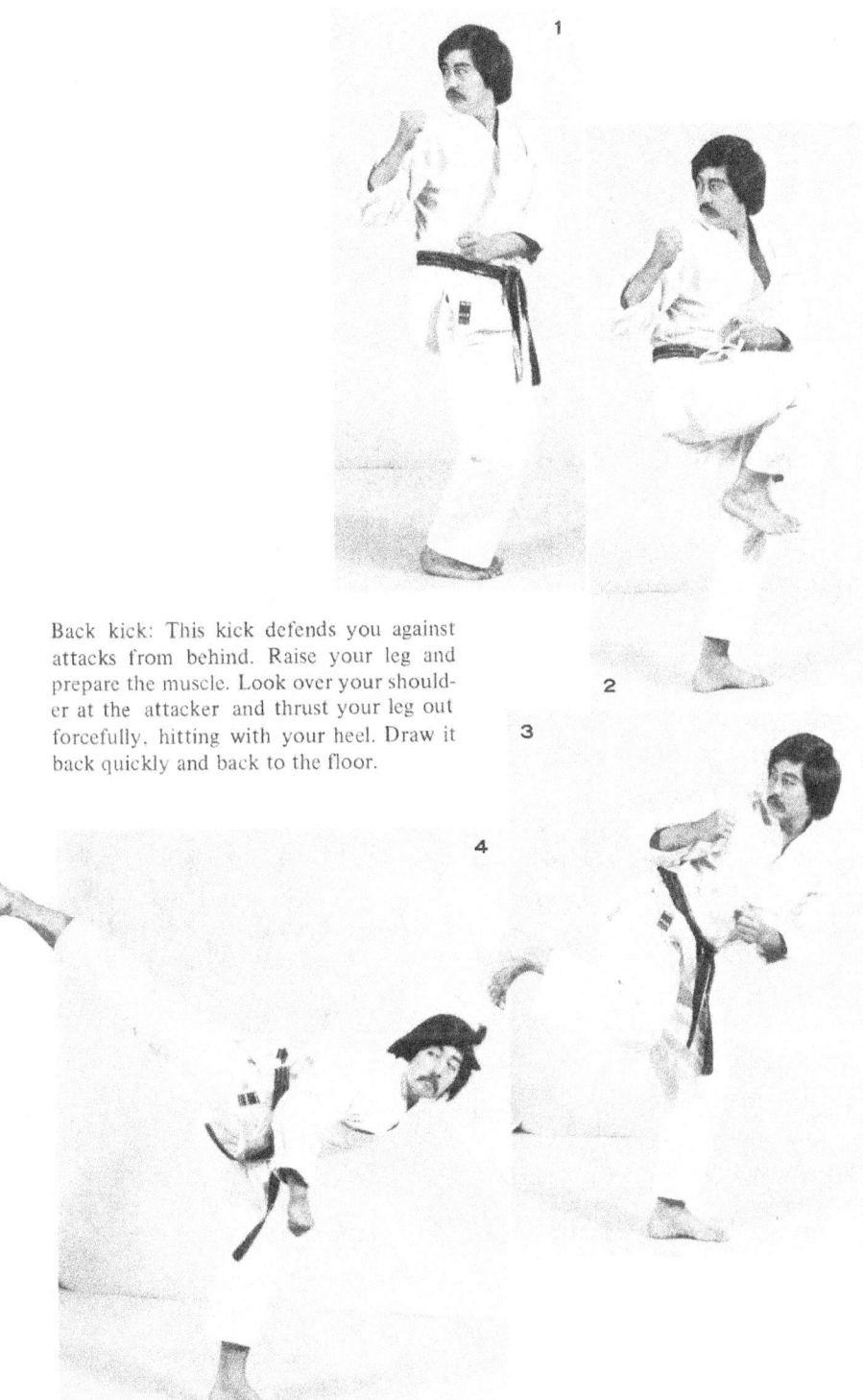

Back kick: This kick defends you against attacks from behind. Raise your leg and prepare the muscle. Look over your shoulder at the attacker and thrust your leg out forcefully, hitting with your heel. Draw it back quickly and back to the floor.

Blocking

Much practice is required to increase your timing and accuracy in blocking rapid punches or kicks. It is important to remember that while your arm is in motion making the block, you must also move your body. Shift out of range of attacks as an added precaution. The point of these actions is to get away from a blow and then be able to reply with your own counterattack.

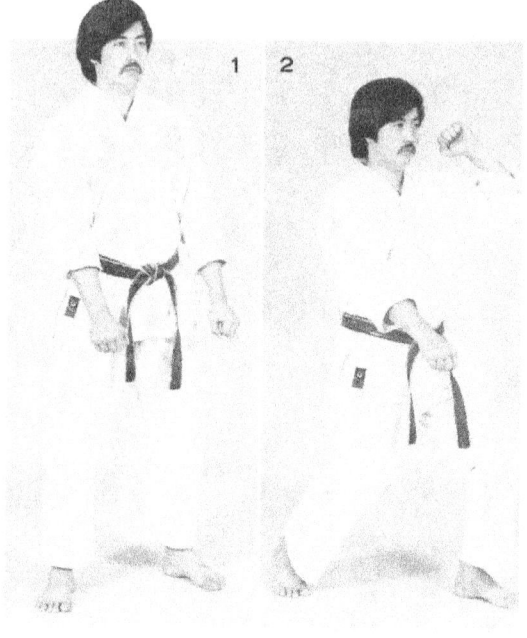

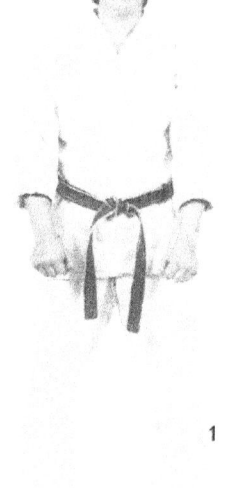

Sweep block:
1. Take a normal position.
2. Begin retreating, back straight, and raise your blocking hand.
3. Begin sweeping downward across the body.
4. Complete as illustrated, punch deflected to side.

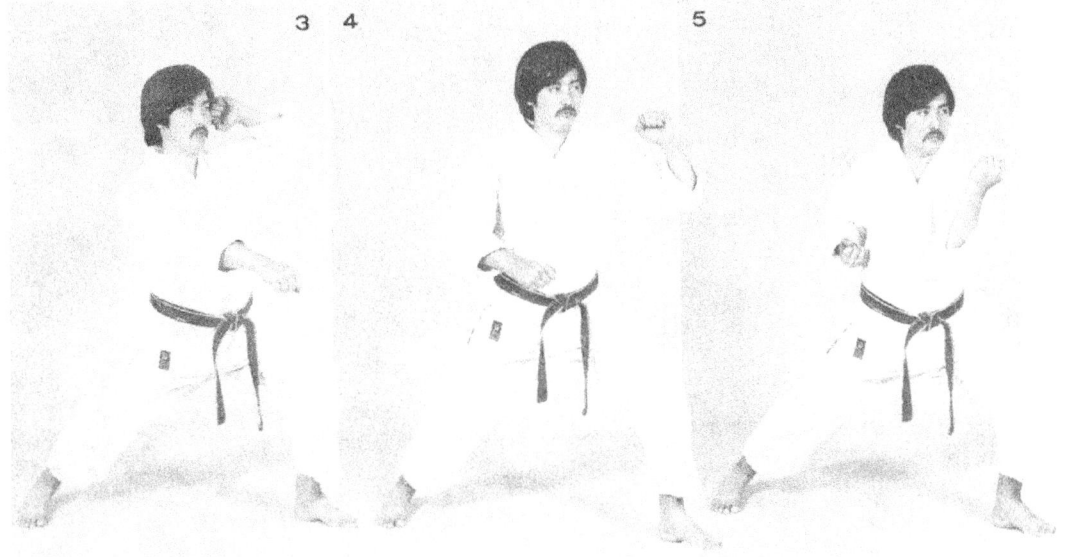

Forearm block:
1. Take a normal position.
2. Begin drawing back, bringing your arm up.
3. If fast enough, you can raise your arm high and come down on the punching arm with great force. Use the bone edge of your arm to do the most damage.
4,5. Snap the block into position, deflecting punch past your body.

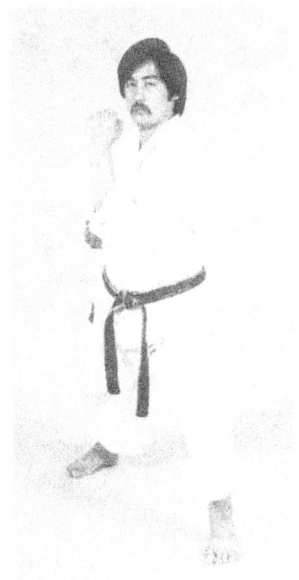

Front View.

Upward block:
1. Take a normal position.
2. Start drawing away from punch, as illustrated.
3. Begin upward thrust of forearm.
4. Complete block as shown, arm at an angle, hitting into the punch with the bone edge of your blocking arm.

Inside forearm block:
1. Stand in a natural position.
2. Begin to draw away from the attack.
4. Your entire forearm acts as a shield.
5. Block with the bone edge of your forearm, deflecting outward.

Knife hand block:
1. Stand in a natural position.
2. Slide back into the Back Stance.
3. Your blocking hand draws up near your ear and starts sweeping outward toward the punch.
4. The entire surface of arm and hand is used to block.
5. Catch or stop the punch on the knife edge of your hand.

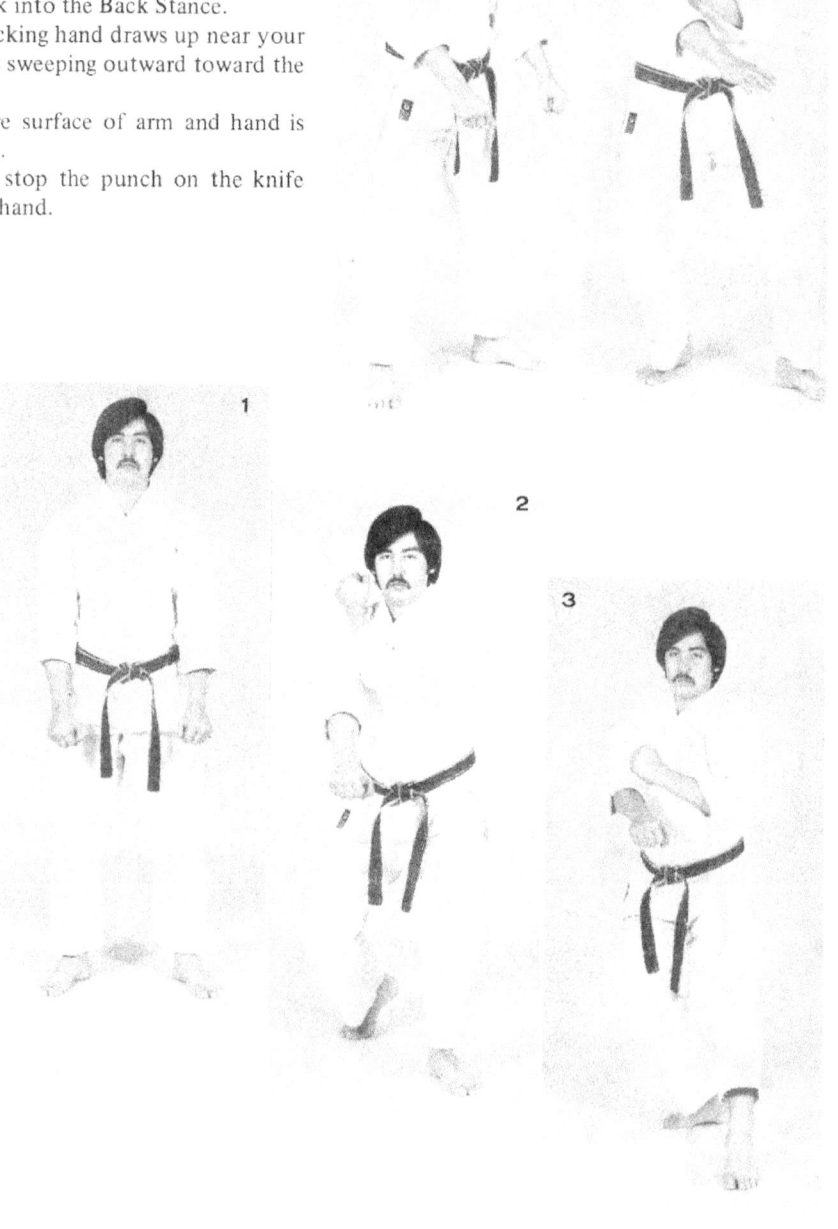

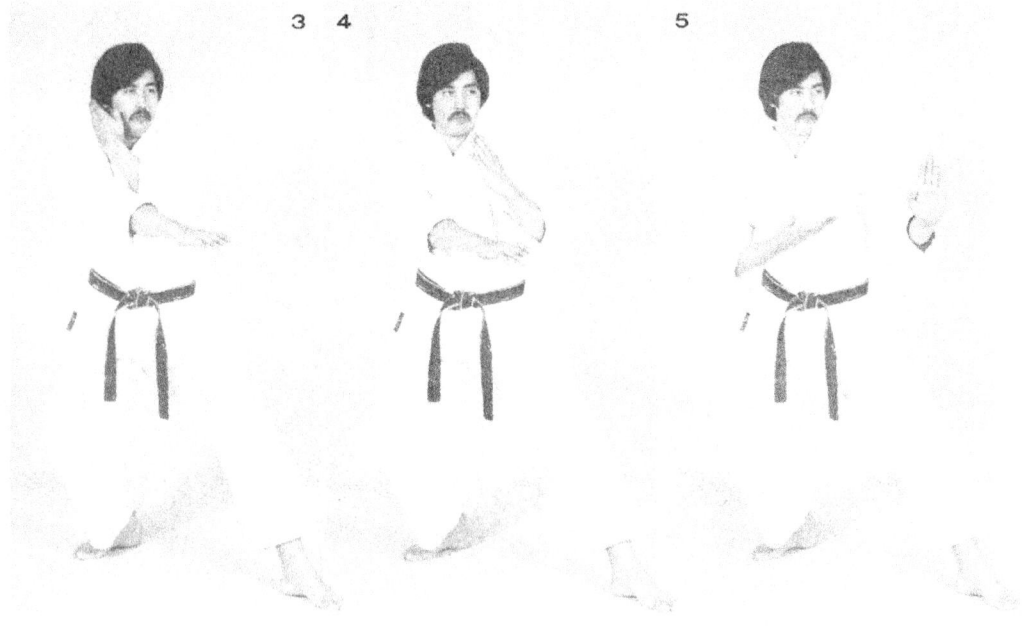

Down block:
1. Stand in a natural stance.
2. Start pulling back, and raise your arm up to your face.
3. Move the raised arm in a downward path, blocking across the body.
4. Complete the block by hitting with the outer edge of your arm and deflecting a LOW PUNCH or KICK to the outside of your body.

Inside forearm down block:
1. Stand in a natural stance.
2. Begin pulling back away from the attack, bring arm to ready as shown.
3. Using the inside of your forearm, deflect across your body.
4. The block is positioned as shown, defending against kicks or low blows.

X-block low:
Performed as illustrated, this block is used against kicks or very low blows.

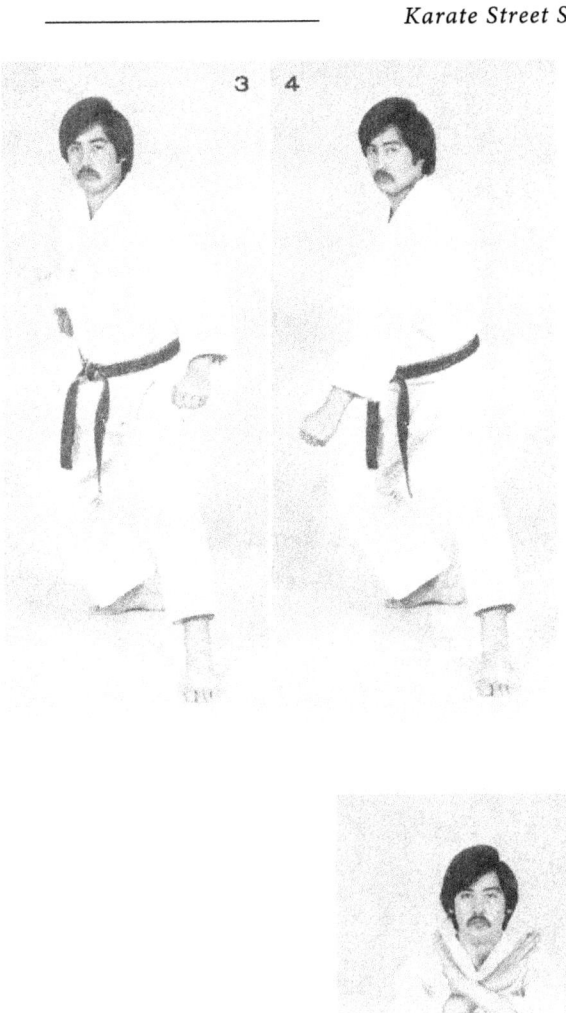

X-block:
Performed as illustrated, this block is used against overhand or high punches. The added protection of both arms stops the blow.

Karate Sparring

In Karate the term sparring refers to practice between two men in which they attack and defend against each other. Because of the dangerous results from actually landing bare hand blows and kicks, the attacks (especially counterattacks) are pulled fractions of an inch short of contact. Needless to say, you would hospitalize most of your opponents if you were to gouge their eyes or kick their groins. All of your attacks are prearranged. To practice defense against face attacks, for example, you ask your partner to punch to the face, then you apply a block and counterattack. To practice properly you must ask the attacker to come at you forcefully and to lunge deeply. This will make you move your entire body. Start slowly, learn to keep your balance, and to keep your eye on your opponent. Build strong counter techniques and strive for maximum speed. Combine your counters so you can effectively use your arms or legs, making it more difficult for an attacker to withstand your barrage of blows.

Face punch defense I:
1. Assume a natural stance.
2. Opponent lunges in with a face punch. Apply an upward block.
3,4,5. Execute a series of counterattacks as you see the openings.

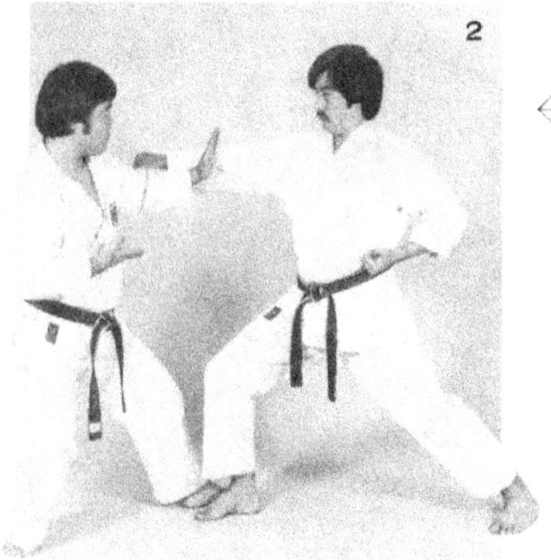

Face punch defense II:
1. Assume a natural stance.
2. Apply your knife block against the punch, using the back stance this time.
3. Grasp and counterkick.
4. Place kicking leg on the floor and gouge at your opponent's face and eyes.
5. Apply a leg sweep. Your leg hooks his from behind and drives him to the ground.
6. Make sure your opponent doesn't get back up.

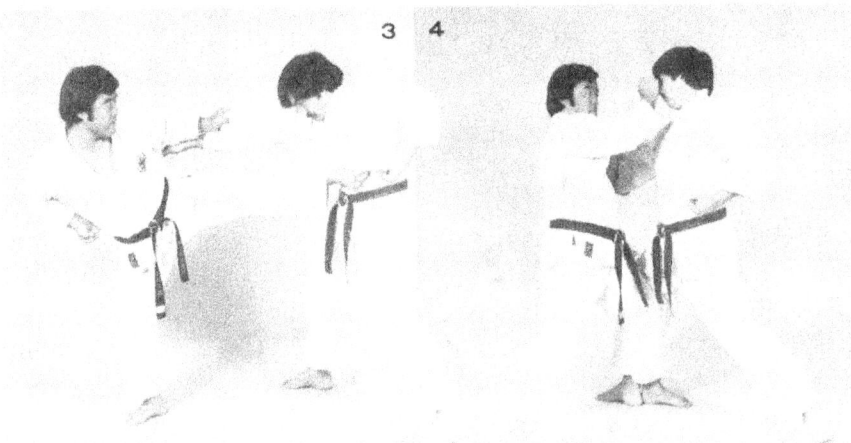

Face punch Defense III:
1. Assume a natural stance.
2. Use an inside forearm block, shifting away from the attack.
3. Grasp the punching arm and counter with a side thrust kick.
4. Follow this with a bottom fist strike to the face.
5. Adjust your position and use your leg to pull or sweep him down from the inside. As you pull his leg up, give him a shove or blow to knock him down.
6. Follow up.

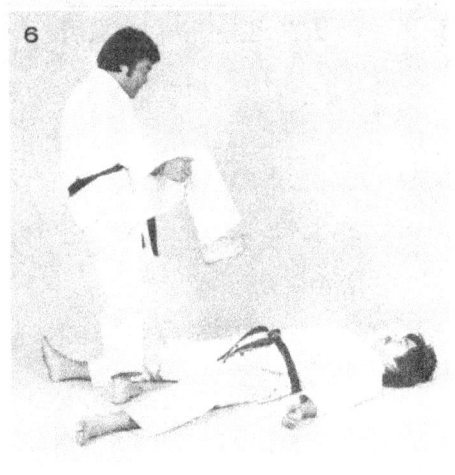

Punch defense:
1. Use a sweep block against your opponent's face or upper body punch. Deflect it past you as shown.
2. Drive a counterpunch up into the exposed rib cage.
3. Pivot your body into an elbow smash to the head.
4. You can sweep or kick his legs out from under him. Sweeps or throws usually come after a blow. This is to soften them up and make them more vulnerable to take-down techniques.
5. Follow up.

Face punch defense IV:
1. Assume a natural stance.
2. Perform an inside forearm block, drawing back into the Cat stance.
3. *FOR A SECOND PUNCH FROM YOUR ATTACKER*, come across with the same blocking arm. On double punch attacks by an opponent, the block arm has only to travel inches across your face for defense. Practice using one hand to block both punches.
4. Counters should be applied before your opponent throws too many attacks. Since it is difficult to stand and block blow after blow, you must counterattack to throw the attacker into a defense position.
5. Quick effective counters will stop an attacker.

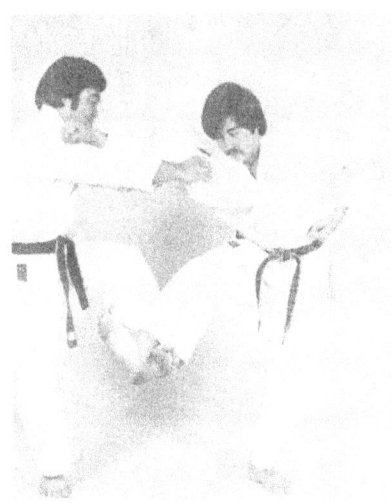 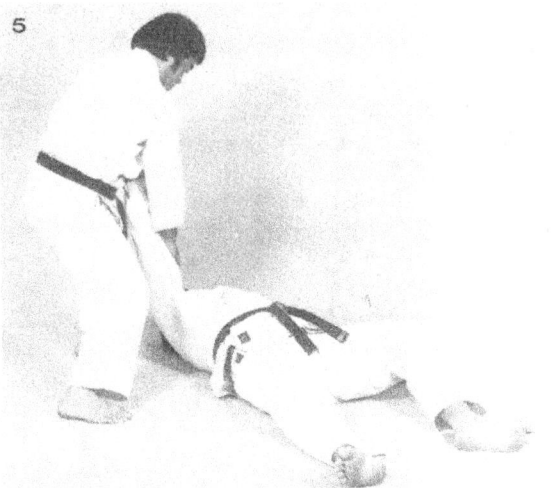

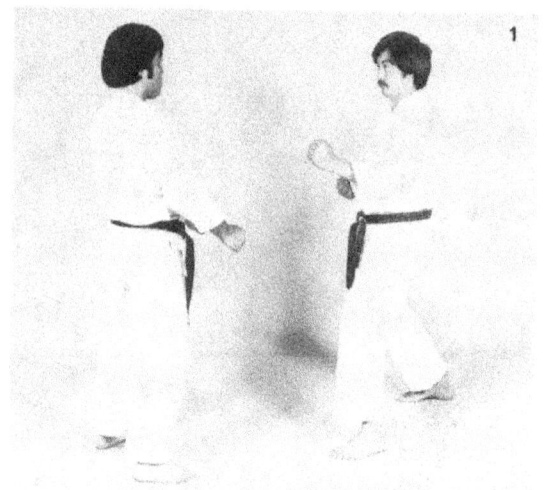

Defense against kick 1:
1. Assume a natural stance.
2. Pull back and away from the force of the kick. Use the forearm block and side stance.
3. When opponent is turned from you as a result of your deflecting block, reach for his head using a punch or palm heel strike.
4. Strike a blow up and into his groin. Grasp groin and clothing firmly.
5. Drive opponent head first to the ground.

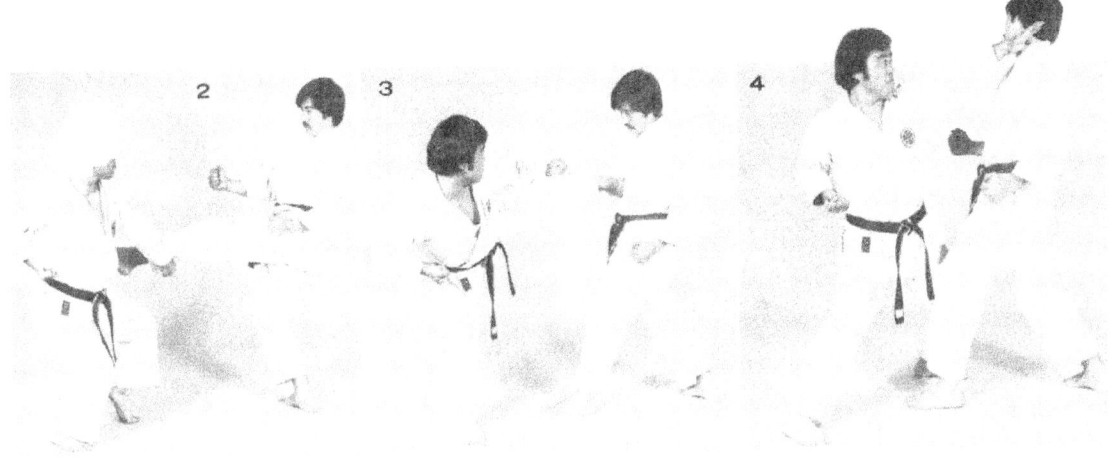

Defense against a kick 2:
1. Assume a natural stance.
2. Block your opponent's kick by shifting sideways into a cat stance, and using a downward block with the arm.
3. As your opponent's forward movement comes to a stop, counterkick with a roundhouse kick.
4, 5. Continue to follow up as necessary.

6. A sweep is applied when you find your leg close to his.

7. Kneel on your opponent's back for control.

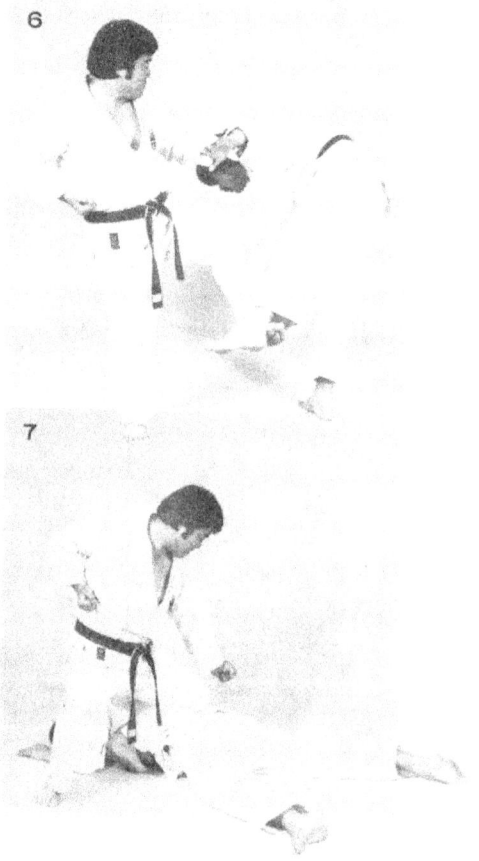

Aiki-do

Aiki-do is a Japanese defense art that was conceived by now-deceased master Morihei Ueshiba. For the layman, Aiki-do is a grappling-type art of defense as compared to the hitting-striking Karate action. Although this is probably not a fair analysis of the noble art of Aiki-do, it is necessary to be brief. It would take volumes of material to delve into the intricate and significant physical and psychological benefits of this art. Master Ueshiba was an exponent of many of the traditional martial arts of Japan during his lifetime, including Judo, Ju-jitsu, Kendo (Japanese fencing), Iai-do (swordsmanship), even Karate and some other now obscure arts. Jui-jitsu, which is the application of leverage, throwing, pressure points, arm and wrist locks, etc. obviously influenced Master Ueshiba the most in devising Aiki-do. Above all, he was deeply religious and a humanitarian. Therefore his techniques rely heavily on evasive action against aggression. Retaliatory blows are practically nonexistent in Aiki-do. Rather, the purpose is to cause submission or discourage attackers by simply escaping, or if necessary, applying minimal pressure or leverage to cause defeat. Notwithstanding this fact, there are disguised in the format of Aiki-do's passive resistance numerous defense techniques that are extremely powerful and effective.

At the risk of offending some alumni, we have extracted techniques of Aiki-do that are practical to use for self-defense in the street. Time and space do not permit us to give more detailed explanations of the foot patterns and intricate leverages Aiki-do offers.

Arm bar:
1. Your opponent grasps your lapel.
2. Pull back to put him off balance holding him securely to you with both hands.
3. Pivot your body as shown, bringing your elbow over his. Both your hands grip as illustrated.
4. Force his elbow down, pulling his hand up to create better leverage. If necessary you can drop your opponent face down on the floor or merely apply pressure until he submits.
5. Close examination will reveal the added pressure to opponent's wrist. Clamp the elbow to your side and pull the hand back hard, creating leverage at the wrist.

5

4

3

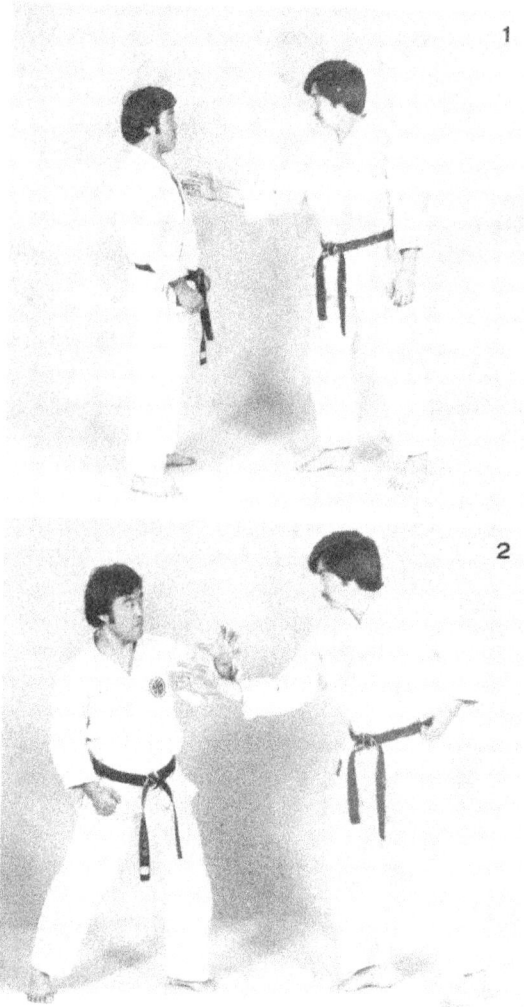

Outside wrist take-down:
1. Your opponent reaches for you.
2. Pivot back, bringing your hand up to grab his.
3. Grasp with your fingertips in his palms, your thumbs on the back of his hand.
4. Support this grab with your other hand, also with your fingertips in palms, thumbs on back of his hand.
5. Examine the hand position closely. Twist your body into the hand and wrist action.

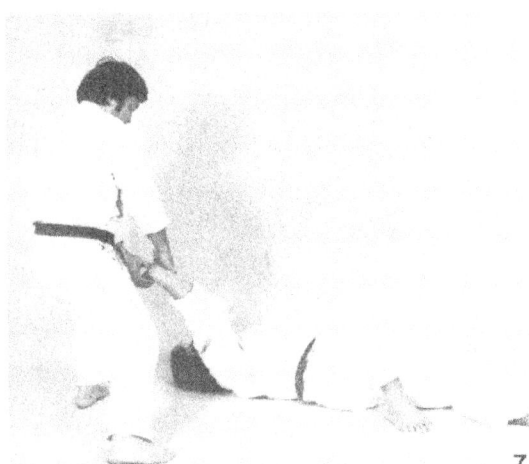

6. Twist deeply to the outside, pressure on the wrist. Direct his fingertips back toward him, or pull outward from the body, two slightly different ways of dropping him to the ground.

7. Opponent ends up on his back. In the Police section the officer used a similar technique and then forced the opponent over on his stomach.

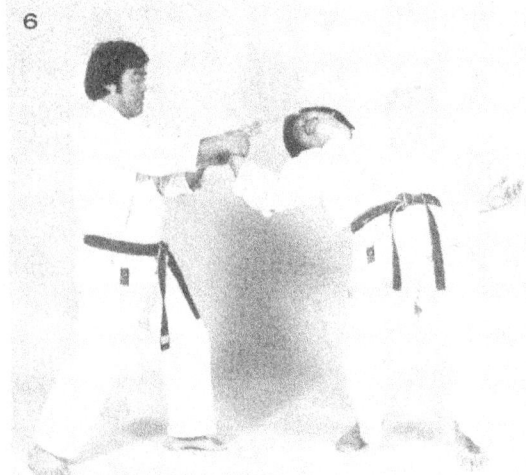

Two-hand wrist grab:
1. Opponent grabs both your wrists.
2. Twist your hands inward, fingertips pointing up. You will be twisting against his thumbs.
3. Examine the grip closely. You come under with one of your hands and grasp him—fingertips over, thumb digging into his palm. Your thumb is on the back of his hand.
4. Your other hand grabs over the top of his, again with your fingertips in his palm, thumbs on the back of his hand. Applying strength with both your hands, twist outward.
5. The resulting pressure will produce the leverage to drop him to the ground.

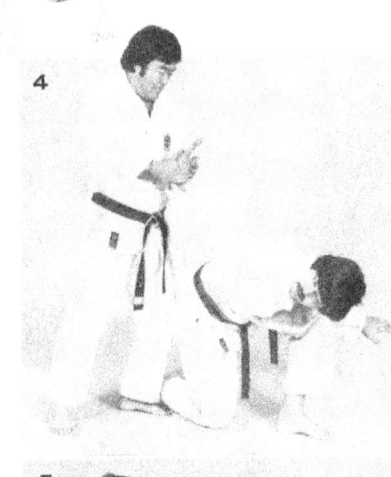

Reverse wrist take down:
1. Your opponent reaches for you.
2. Pivot your leg back and around as shown, reaching over his hand with yours.
3. Grasp with fingertips in his palms, your thumbs on the back of his hands.
4. To further upset your opponent's balance pull your other leg back (illustration shows your right leg). Your other hand will also grab with fingers in his palm, thumb on back of his hand.
5. Leverage against the wrist can force him face down.

Discouraging a grab 1:
1. An opponent standing to your side grabs at your wrist.
2. With your free hand, clamp his hand against your arm so he can't free his grip. Drop your body weight for leverage and bring your ELBOW up over his forearm.
3. Pulling your elbow backward, holding it close to the body, will cause extreme pressure against his wrist.

Note:
All Aiki-do pressures can cause extreme pain, and even break the joint to which they are applied. Use as much pressure as necessary to throw your opponent down. With practice, you will be able to decide how hard the technique must be applied.

Discouraging a grab 2:
1. Your opponent reaches out and grasps your wrist.
2. Reach over with your free hand and grab his wrist. Start to slide in with your leg.
3. Come in low and close to him. Holding firm with your grabbing hand, apply pressure to his fingers and wrist by pushing the hand that he grabbed.
4. The illustration shows you pulling with one hand and pushing with the other. Study his wrist position carefully.

Evade and choke:
1. Your opponent reaches or punches at you.
2. Parry his hand away from you as you drop back.
3. In an outside circular motion, push his arm out, down and around. It must be one continuous motion, drawing a large circle.
4. Now slide your arm under his while he is off balance.
5. Slide in partially behind him and reach up behind him with your other hand.
6. Apply pressure by clasping your hands together and squeezing his neck and arm together in a vise-like action. You can hold him here, helpless, or squeeze and render him unconscious, or throw him to the ground.

Sacrifice throw:
1. Your opponent attacks with forward momentum.
2. As he steps in, you drop back (block or grab at his arm). A backhand blow to the rib cage will distract or soften him up if necessary.
3. Drop to one knee (therefore the term "sacrifice"). Not resisting his power, you are dropping under it, remaining in complete control. Pulling on his arm, you can grab at his ankle.

4. With your arms outspread, roll him over your back and shoulder muscle, pulling with one arm and lifting with the other. Your opponent will dive face first into the ground or come out of it with a roll, landing on his back.

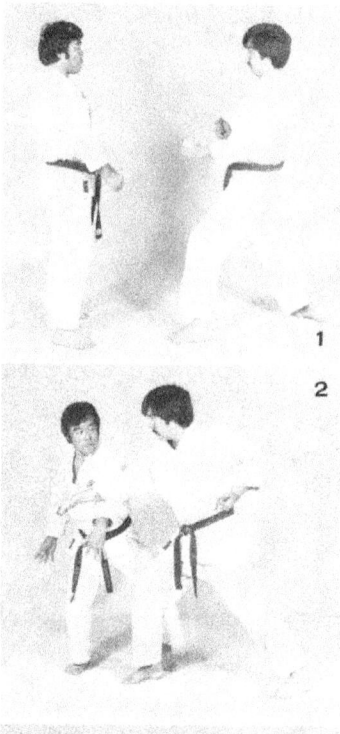

Block and throw:
1. Opponent will lunge in with attack.
2. Pull back and away from the attack, turning to face as shown in illustration. Your arm will block or deflect his.
3. Your left leg may have to slide behind his, as your blocking arm lifts up under his.
4. Twist your body toward him, bringing one arm up under his chin and striking or pushing across his stomach with your other arm. Your leg is now a solid brace behind him. Study the arm positions. He is bent, helpless. The arm up under the chin and hand across his stomach can either push or hit forcefully, depending on the damage you wish to do.
5, 6. Continue twisting your body around against his, dropping to your knee for balance. This will throw him to the ground, on his back.

Judo

Judo was for years the favorite martial art of the Japanese people. It was the child of Professor Jigoro Kano, now deceased, who's legacy spans the world. The Kodokan Judo Institute in Tokyo, Japan, mecca for Judo practitioners of all races, was Professor Kano's headquarters. Here, in the formative years, the small but powerful Kano took on all comers in bare-hand contests. An upstart in the established Ju-jitsu community, Kano had to physically prove himself and the art that he termed Judo, the 'gentle way'. Being a nation of swordsmen, the Japanese practiced techniques of unarmed defense that were related to sword action. This was called Ju-jitsu and existed for centuries. Ju-jitsu was, and still is today, an outstanding method of self-defense. Our own military and the militaries of other nations base their armies', unarmed combat techniques on the art of Ju-jitsu. This art includes not only leverage, pressure, balance, and throwing, but also hitting, gouging and kicking. From his boyhood days, Kano studied and refined the techniques of Ju-jitsu, seeking out masters from across the length of Japan. He decided, after many years of training to combine some of Ju-jitsu techniques, eliminate others, and add some of his own to devise the art of Judo. His purpose was to make a combat sport that all ages could practice. Prior to that, only the Samurai and fight-oriented Japanese practiced Ju-jitsu. The moves Kano instituted for Judo could be practiced repeatedly and with abandon. One no longer had to stop short of breaking an opponent's arm or leg. Now in Judo one could freely have contests to see which man could throw the other. Soon Judo was accepted by the Japanese schools, and tournaments and exhibitions were promoted. The purpose of Judo then became one of sport, and that is how it remains today. Judo is a sport that attracts competitors from almost every nation of the world. If you are well-trained in Judo, regardless of its sporting aspect, you will have the skill to quickly smash an opponent to the ground on his back, his head, or even choke him into unconciousness. Perhaps you could throw an arm bar on him that will have him cringing in pain. Sport or not, with some adaptation, Judo can add to your knowledge of self-defense for the street.

Throws

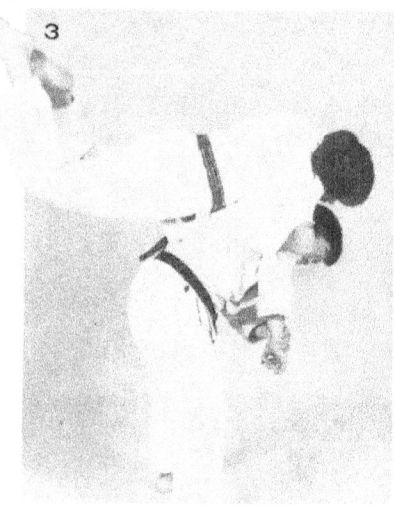

Shoulder throw:
1. Grasp opponent's arm and step in across his body.
2. Fit your upper arm and shoulder under his armpit. Bring your other leg around into position so that you now face in the same direction as he. Squat low and fit your body snugly to his and pull him forward off balance, grasping with both hands as shown.
3. Throw him over your shoulder and back by RAISING with your legs and pulling him forward.
4, 5. Illustrates the completion of throw.
For self-defense:
This particular throw can be applied when an opponent grabs you from behind.

Foot sweep:
1. Grasping your opponent's arm, slide around slightly to his side.
2. Bring your foot around behind his heel.
3. Sweep or raise his leg with your foot, while pulling his arm to get him off balance.
4. Kick your foot high and pull hard on the arm.
5. This will throw him hard to the ground on his back.

Self defense:
When an attacker advances on you with one leg forward, you can sweep or kick it out from under him.

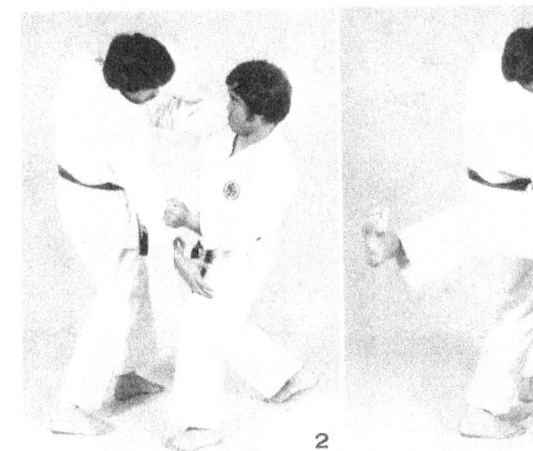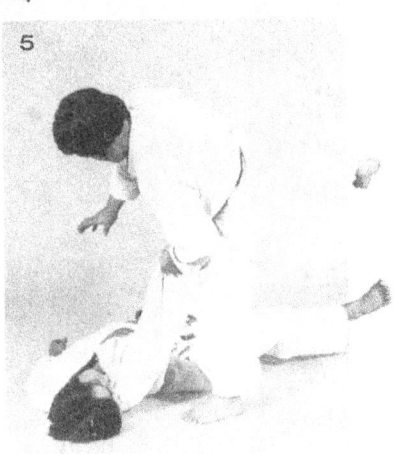

Leg sweep:
1. Grab his arm and lapel.
2. Pull him off balance.
3. Step in close to him and with your leg raised high behind him, prepare to sweep it out from under him.
4. Throw your body into it, and in a hard sweeping motion, chop his leg out from under him.
5. This will drive an opponent hard to the ground.

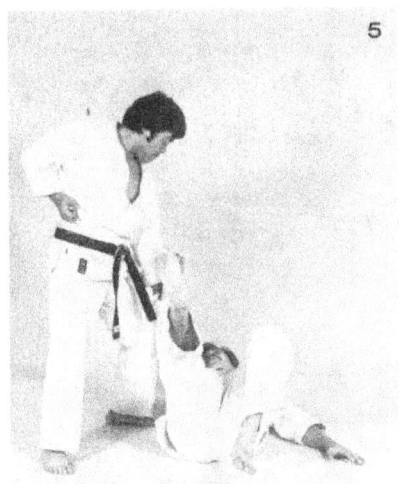

Self-defense:
This technique is used by the police because of its effectiveness and simplicity of application.

Inside leg sweep:
1. Grasp your opponent with both hands, and slide your foot in between his legs.
2. Hook your foot behind his leg, low at his ankle for best leverage.
3. Pull his leg forward and out from under him as you push.
4. Push hard and lean into the throw, dropping him on his back.

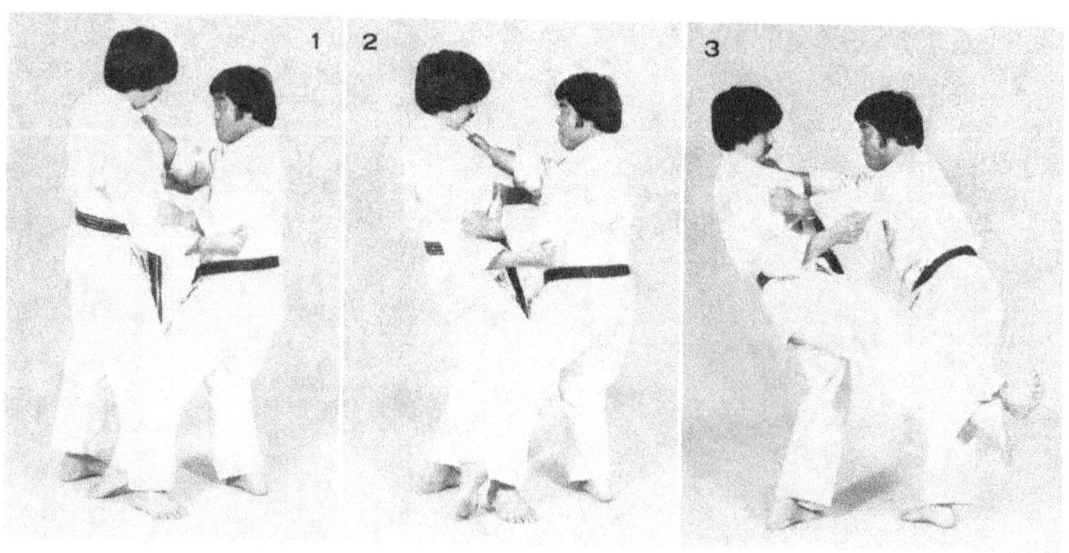

←

Hip throw:
Self-defense:
This can be done when someone approaches from behind or grapples with you.
1. Step in and across your opponent's body, one arm circling his waist, the other holding his arm.
2. Pivot your other leg into position and fit your hips snugly to his lower body. Drop your weight, squat low, and pull him tightly against you.
3. Throw by twisting and raising with the legs.
4. This will throw him over your hip to the ground on his back.

Self-defense:
If an attacker comes in close to you with his legs spread wide, you can slide in quickly and pull one of his legs out from under him.

Drop and roll:
1. Grasp your opponent and slide one leg in between his.
2. Sit quickly on the ground and place your foot on his stomach.
3. Pull hard, rolling back, and kick him up and over with your leg. This should be done in one continuous motion.
4. Your opponent will come out landing on his back.

Self-defense:
When an attacker overpowers you or lunges at you, get a hold on him and drop. Use the power of you legs to throw him over. If you miss the throw at least you can kick his groin or stomach from here.

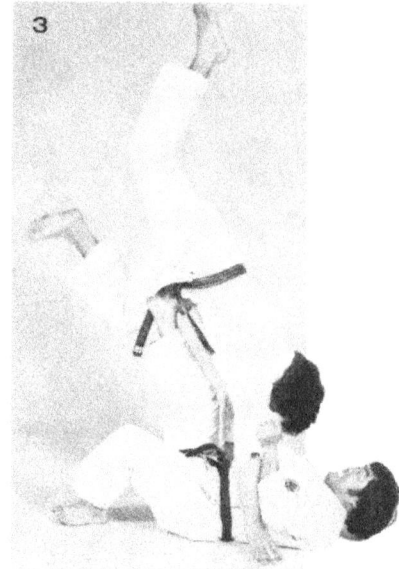

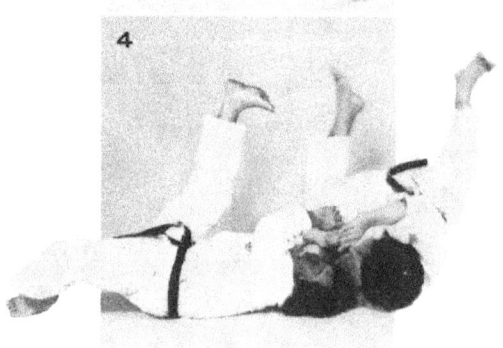

Chokes

Choke:
1. Bring your arm around your opponent's neck, your forearm across the throat.
2. Clasp your hands together and pull back, creating a vise action.

Self-defense:
Used frequently in police agencies under emergency conditions, this is one of the few ways to subdue a man under the influence of a pain-killing narcotic. It is very dangerous, and can cause serious injury or death if applied too hard.

Front cross choke:
1. When in front of an opponent, reach across and grab his clothing.
2. Reach up under his lapel with your other hand.
3. One hand pulls down and the other forearm bars across his throat for pressure.

Self-defense:
When in a wrestling situation, standing or on the ground, your forearm pushes up across his throat. Very dangerous if applied too hard.

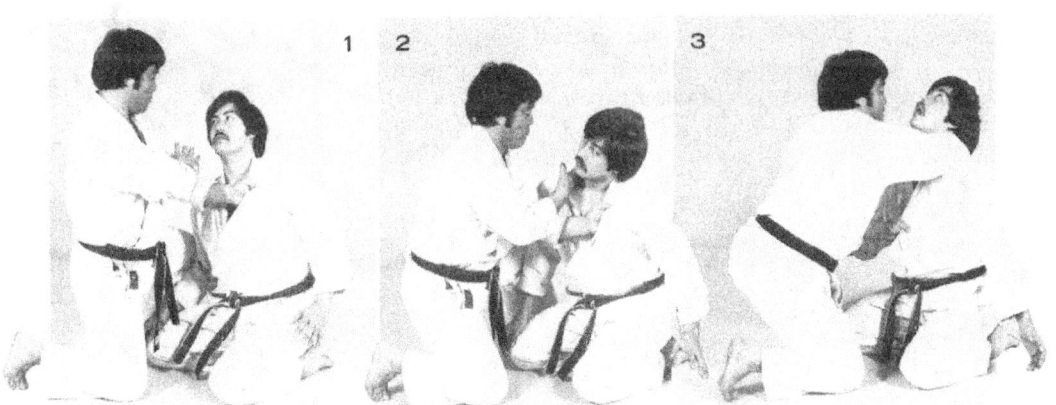

Rear choke:
1. Reach around your opponent.
2. Pull down on his clothing with one hand.
3. Your other hand encircles his neck and grasps his clothing for leverage.
4. Pull back with forearm bar across the throat.

Self-defense:
This is a bit more difficult than the first choke given in this section. Again, pressure against the throat is very dangerous.

Bar and choke:
1. Bring one arm around your opponent's neck.
2. Place the other arm forward so that your opposite hand can grasp your inside elbow.
3. Place this hand behind his head as illustrated.
4. Push head foward and bar his throat as shown.

Self-defense:
Again, this is an extremely dangerous hold to apply, the double pressure of both your arms making it possibly one of the most lethal of the chokes. VERY EASY TO CAUSE SERIOUS INJURY OR DEATH.

Falls

Falling and rolling:
You can fall to the ground, even on hard concrete, and come out of it with little more than bruises. Of first concern in falling is protecting the head, since head injuries are the most serious. When falling backward, the force of the fall is absorbed in the upper arm and back muscle. Keep the chin tucked in to chest so the back of your head doesn't snap against the ground. Two things that will injure the most are hitting your head and slamming your back squarely on the ground. Hitting hard between the shoulder blades can knock the wind out of you. Thus there is a slight twist as you hit to absorb the blow on your side. SEE PHOTO 6. This is the best way to land after being thrown down or falling. If you must land squarely on the back, hit the ground with both arms to absorb the force into your arms instead of your back.

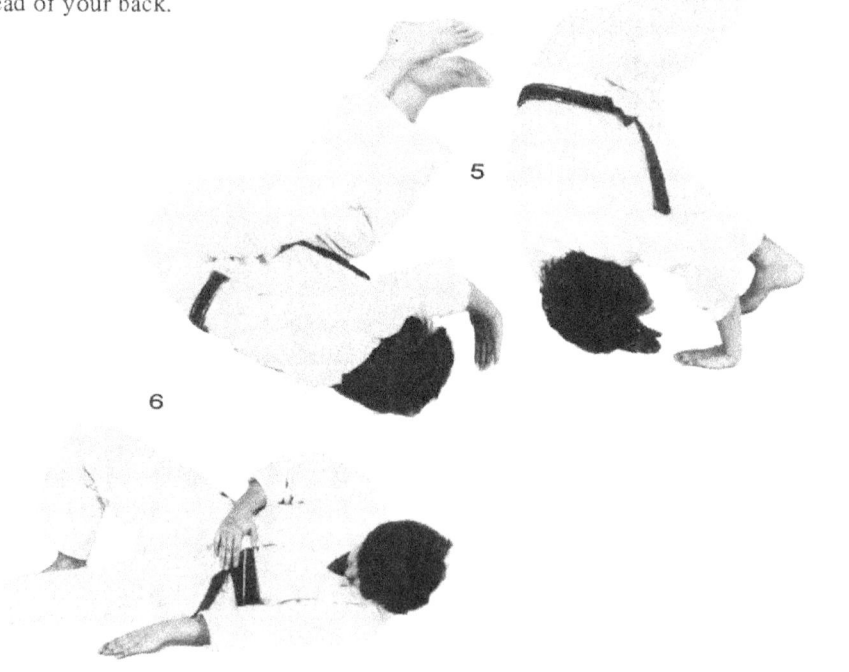

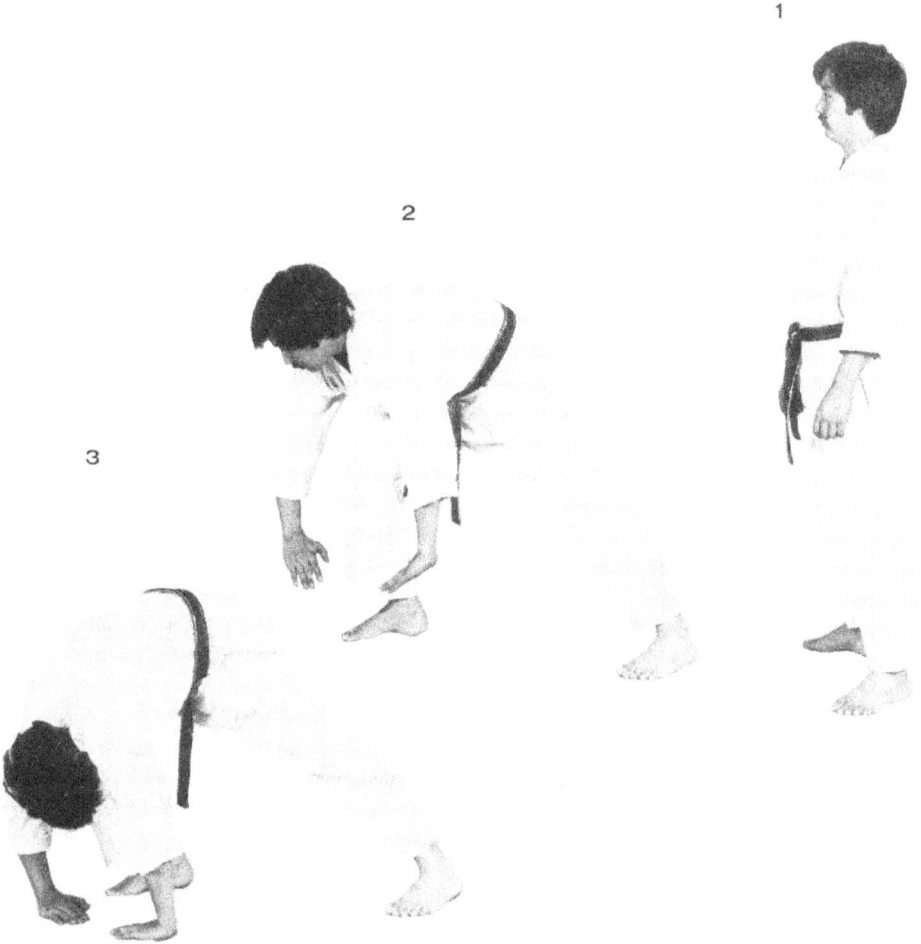

Falling forward:
Illustrations one through six show the proper execution of a forward roll. Your arms make a circle and protect the head. The roll is over the outer edge of your arm and over your back, head tucked in. If you land face first, flatten out and slide on the stomach and arms. Watch a baseball player sliding into base. In falling forward, the point is not to injure the head or face.

Exercises

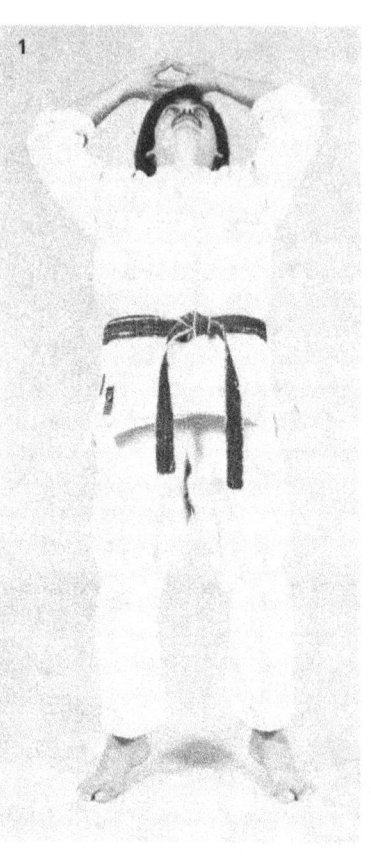

Keeping fit is just good common sense. If your body is in shape, you stand a better chance of protecting yourself in the street. Should you never have to defend yourself, keeping fit is still important for maintaining good health. Here are some basic exercises; they take only a few minutes and can be done anywhere. Most martial arts use these exercises as they are important for keeping supple.

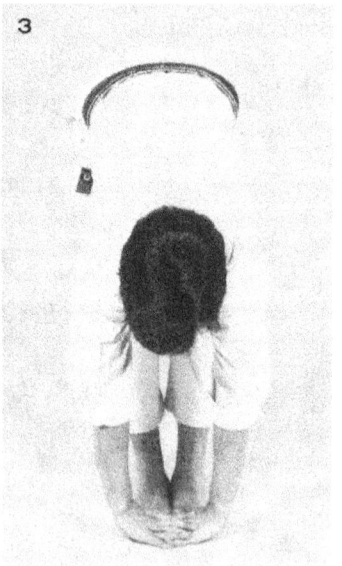

1. Stretch. Reach high and backward.
2. Body twisting. Twist as far as you can in both directions.
3. Touching the floor. Keep the knees from bending and work toward touching the hands to the floor.
4. Leg and hip stretch. Squat as shown and work on the leg.
5. Squat and stretch the leg muscle. Sit on one leg and extend the other. Bounce up and down from here.
6. Sit with both legs in front of you and pull your head to your knees.

When doing these exercises, remember that it takes time for the muscle to warm up so take a minute or two with each set, working into the position slowly.

Karate Street Survival

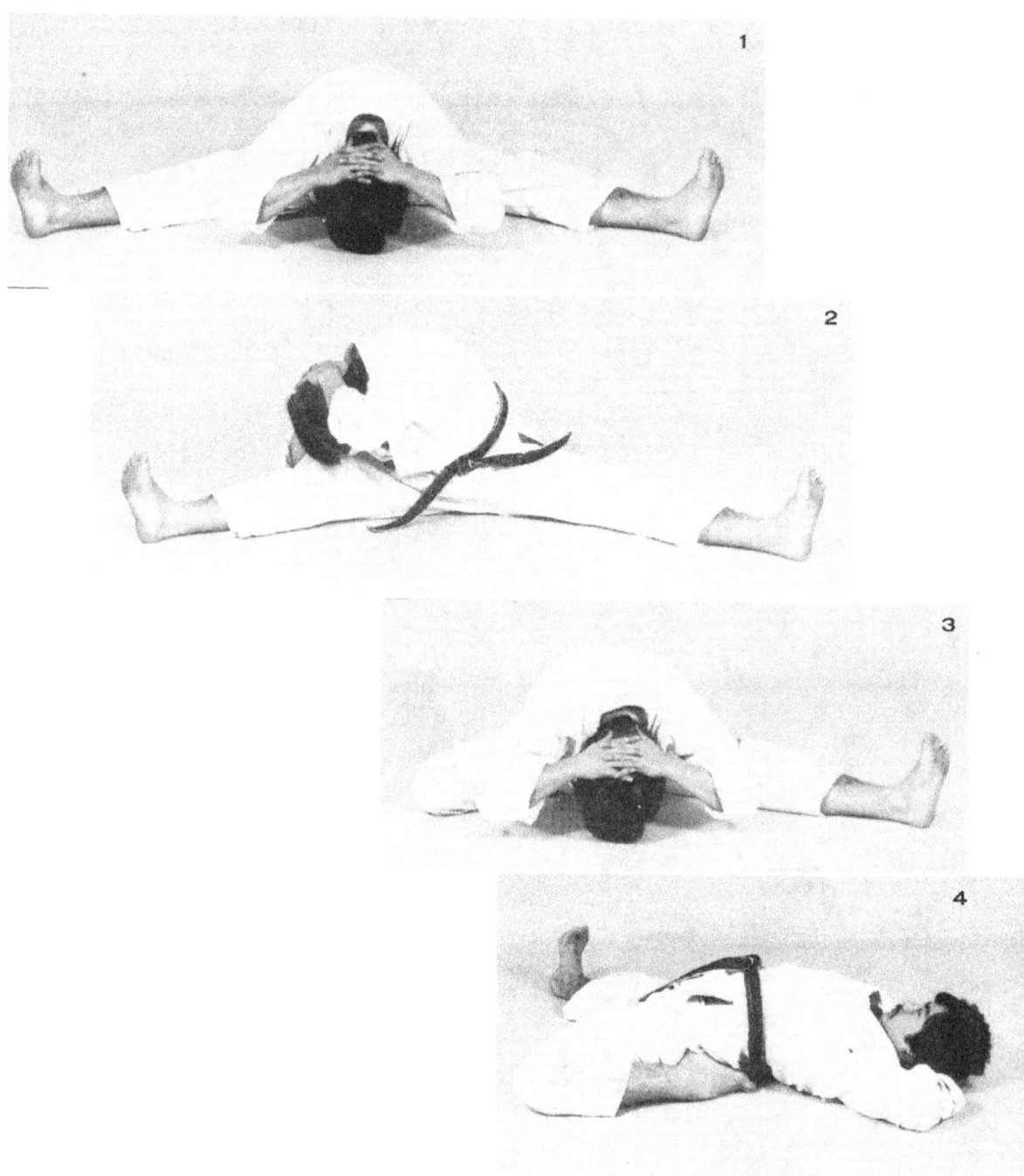

148

Stretching the leg muscles:
Staying loose and supple in the legs gives you better balance and footwork when defending yourself. You can also kick faster and stronger. Above all you want to avoid getting stiff and awkward. Since we travel by car so frequently, our legs no longer get the exercise they need. Here are some stretches that will benefit you in many ways.

1. Spread your legs wide and touch the floor with your head. This takes time, so give yourself a few minutes to warm up and get the blood flowing. Sit straight up and then bend to the floor, repeatedly.
2. This time touching either leg, repeat the above exercise.
3. In another variation, fold one leg back under you.
4. Sit back while leg is folded.
5. Fold both legs and sit back. This one seems to be hard for many, so we suggest you hold yourself with your arms on the floor behind you and, little by little, lower yourself each day until you can do it.
6. Place your feet together and force your knees downward.

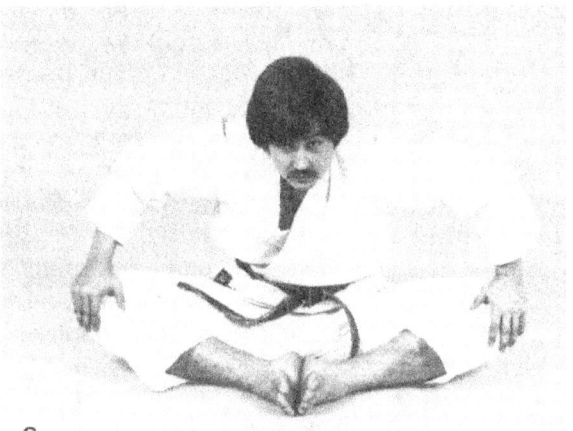
6

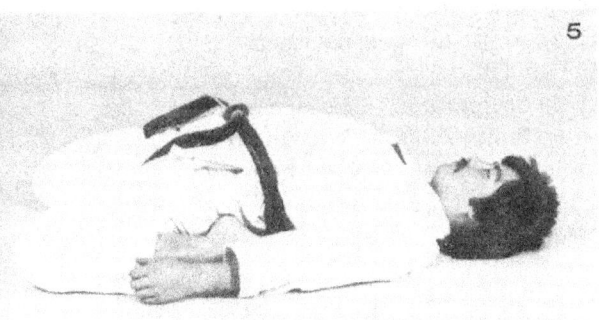
5

Psychological Strategies against Attack or Rape

Defenses against Attack

The other chapters of this book demonstrated techniques to be used in violent street encounters. They deal with your *physical* response to danger. This chapter, instead, focuses on the *psychological* side of surviving an encounter with a mugger, assailant, or rapist. Here are some important points to always remember to apply anytime you may be targeted as a victim by an assailant. The most dangerous weapon you have is your own mind. Try to never lose or let go of your ability to keep thinking, planning, and working out strategies to stay alive and fit. The moment you let go and allow panic, terror, or even blind rage to take over, you have markedly reduced your chance of surviving. This does not mean you are supposed to be in control of the situation, but in control of yourself. For example, you may decide that the best thing to do in a dangerous encounter, at that moment, is absolutely nothing at all. But *keep thinking and scheming to survive.*

The next important point has to do with you and the law, if you have used lethal force against an attacker or rapist. It used to be that a criminal who attempted to use force against an honest citizen, and was hurt or killed in the try, was thought to have gotten what he deserved. Today, this is not so. With the increased interest of the courts in individual rights, a criminal defense can be based on arguments that, when successful, seem travesties of justice. So remember, if you decide to use lethal force against an attacker or rapist, you *could* face legal consequences. A good rule of thumb that is simple enough to keep in mind and remember, even in the mind-numbing stress of lifethreatening encounter, is to *use no more force than is necessary to end the attack.* If you overstep this, you may be taken into court later. But as a Texas sheriff once said, it's far, far better to be the one going to court than the one that's dead.

Another important point is, an ounce of prevention is *not* worth a pound of cure, *it is worth your own life.* Crime statistics for big cities show that, if you live in any large urban or suburban area, you are wrong if you think it "can't happen to me." Based on the statistics, you will be the victim of a robbery, mugging, murder, or rape *at least once* in your life. *So plan for it.* For example, if you go into an area notorious for mugging or rape, plan to park your car in a well-lighted area. Try to take a friend. Keep all your car doors locked while driving. When on foot, think about what could serve as a weapon in case of attack—umbrellas, brief cases, and so forth. A heavy purse has immobilized many an inept, would-be robber. If you are accosted and end up using unarmed self-defense techniques to protect yourself, check the ground for slickness: Keep in mind that your attacked picked his ground and picked you; do not give him any more edge than he already has Research has shown that victims have a lot in common, even in their walking gait and posture. So do not think and act like a victim; *think and act like a survivor.* Beyond this, the number of factors you can use to avoid violent encounters are almost too numerous to mention. Each person must look to the situations of his or her daily life and work to safeguard themselves.

Surprisingly, one of the most frequent places victims are attacked is in the "safety" of their own home. This is especially true in instances of rape. Many police departments will help you check out your home for possible points of forcible entry. Since it is such a high risk area, a woman should never let a stranger in her home when she is alone. If someone comes to the door and says there is an emergency, offer to telephone for him rather than letting him in. If he refuses this offer, observe him to see where he goes—if he goes next door to a neighbor's home, or tries to find another way into your home. If he acts in a suspicious manner, call the police, and also try to furnish them with a good description of him. Finally, remember you are *nearly* always vulnerable. Be aware that you are at risk, even in a place very familiar to you. And, if you are in strange or unfamiliar surroundings, play a game of imagining how you could be attacked wherever you are, and how you would survive. Try to make this an automatic process. In the end, despite all of these measures, you are still vulnerable. But you can reduce the chances of an attack happening by planning ahead in *countless ways.* And keep in mind, too, that when you are attacked, your thinking is never as clear as it can be before, when you can still *plan ahead.*

Types of Assailants

We can now talk about the kinds of attackers you are most likely to meet, and some counter-strategies that are simple enough to be useful when you find yourself in the stress of the encounter. There are the *professional criminal, aggressive assailant,* and the *crazy or deranged attacker.* The professional criminal is just that, a pro. He is not interested in anything but money. He has one objective, taking your money or property with as little risk to himself as possible. His crimes are generally well planned. He is all business, but do not foolishly assume that this guy will "take your dough and go." Some professional criminals make it a practice of killing the one witness to their crime—their victim!

The aggressive assailant may appear to be after your property, but he's really there to get your person! He makes himself feel better by making you feel worse, so the loot is secondary. For example, an acquaintance of mine from England was attacked in New York's Central Park by two black men with knives. They demanded his wallet. He indignantly refused and said, with his very British accent, *No,* he was a visitor from England, and as a guest in America he resented being robbed. The robbers, surprised by his accent, said, "Oh, we thought you were a white guy." They turned around and walked away. Interracial crimes are often committed for aggressive reasons, rather than for monetary gain.

The deranged or crazy attacker is the poorest planner. His acts are usually not understood by the victim. In newspaper accounts, they are the so-called senseless acts of brutality. They can be the most frightening attackers to their assailants because they seem to have no comprehensible objective. For example, a nurse described such an incident. Her car stalled on the way home from work one night. She was standing, waiting for a tow truck when a man came up from behind, put his arms around her and grabbed her. But when she screamed he became so frightened he let go. He told her he wasn't going to hurt her, and even stood there while she ran to a nearby phonebooth to call the police.

A fourth type of attacker, once rare but becoming more common today, is the terrorist. He is politically motivated, and may see himself as a good person, a savior. His attacks are very well planned. He can be most willing to sacrifice his life *and yours* to reach his objective.

Now that you know something about your attackers, here are some things you should and should not do if faced with an assailant.

Do's and Don'ts for Prospective Victims

First, do not bad mouth your attacker. Do not tell him what a jerk he is. Do not tell him that you are better than he is. Do not threaten to beat him up. Don't even tell him your hands are registered weapons. Above all, do not tell him you will get even with him later. If he is a *professional criminal* you are wasting your time and his, and he may take tougher measures to get what he wants. Remember, you are under intense stress and you may think it will make you feel better to let off a little steam with your mouth, yet, your attacker is also under stress and you strain his patience and *accomplish nothing!* You may even provoke him further if he is an *aggressive assailant*, there to humiliate you. So if you put *him* down you may make him go farther than he planned to put *you* down! And if he is a crazy attacker you may confuse him even more, escalating the chance of it being another senseless act of violence. Threatening your assailant is even worse. It alerts his own protective instincts. Instead, if you talk to him *do so in a calm, firm voice.*

Second, if he wants to talk, then do so. Delaying is time for you. It allows you time to calm down and plan. It also increases the chance someone will stumble on the encounter and discover you two. But *do not stall him.* You may be risking an impatient reprisal.

Third, do not treat the encounter as no big deal, or trivial, or matter-of-factly. It almost certainly is a big deal to the assailant who may be further provoked into showing you that it is a big deal!

Fourth, do not believe the assailant who assures you that he is only after your money, car, body etc. This may be a trick to put you in a more vulnerable position by getting you to drop your defenses. For example, Charles Manson and his followers talked the Tate victims into being tied up by reassuring them that the Manson bunch were robbers only. Manson then proceeded to slaughter Sharon Tate and her guests.

Fifth, if your assailant starts spouting reasons for his actions whether philosophical, political, religious, sociological (e.g., being a member or an economically oppressed class), *listen to his theories and do not tell him that it is the stupidist thing you ever heard.*

You may enrage him. He is telling you his ideas so you can "understand" why you are his victim. He wants you to see him as a person and if he *thinks* you do, he *may* begin to see *you* as more than a victim and increase your survival chances. Likewise, do not act like what he is telling you is the greatest thing you have ever heard, making you ready to become a new convert. He will probably know you are patronizing him and become angered. *Just try to look interested.*

Sixth, do not offer the assailant money. That may offend him or make him feel out of control. If he wants your money he will demand it. In one instance political terrorists killed their hostages after their government offered to buy them off with money. The terrorists were insulted, enraged, and murdered the victims to prove to the government that theirs was a selfless cause.

Seventh, if you decide to protect yourself with a counter attack do it instantaneously and without verbal or nonverbal warning. Mind the motto of combat pistol shooters: *speed, power, accuracy*. Initiate your attack explosively, aim straight for the best area to disable or kill and put as much power into it as you can. Remember nothing enrages an attacker more than an inept, bungled, unsuccessful counter attack. *Make it work* the first and only time because the attacker is not going to give you a second chance to get it right.

Eighth, once you start your counter attack, *continue until you are absolutely sure the attacker is out of action*. Do not strike once; plan multiple attacks. Once you start your attacks, continue until he is down, totally unable to hurt you in any way. Too many times victims deliver one single counter attack, move and do not follow through with others. *Once started, keep your attack coming and coming.*

Ninth, use all the help you can get. Nearly anything can be a weapon *for you* —pencils, pens, shoes, even trash can lids can be put to good use. Slam your attacker against a wall, grab his hair, clothes and slam his head into the cement if you are wrestling with him on the ground.

Tenth, *age, size or sex* of the attacker means nothing. A baby faced, slightly-built teenager with a switch blade knife kills you just as dead as the big two-hundred pounder packing a forty-five. A baby rattlesnake is as lethal as a grown up one. And, violent crime by women are increasing epidemically, so say the statistics. *Treat all assailants as dangerous.*

Defense against Rape

There is no clear, obvious way to classify rapists, especially since speed is a critical factor in such an attack. However, some knowledge of the several kinds of motivation for rape can affect the defensive technique adopted, even within the few seconds available to gauge the attacker's behavior and choose the appropriate response. Familiarizing oneself with the different personality characteristics of rapists is a necessary first step to effective self-defense, just as physical resistance is the last step since it commits you, irrevocably, to deadly force, and the possible crippling or blinding of your assailant. Concern about use of such force does not refer to the rapist but to yourself, because in using violence you determine the attacker's own violent reaction.

In addition to appraising your own lifestyle—evaluating your surroundings and the kinds of risks inherent in them—you can prepare to defend yourself against an actual attack by learning to identify the following personality categories that typify rapists:

Immature Personality: This is usually a young person who has not learned how to form relationships with women or, in most cases, with any of his peers. He does not dislike women. On the contrary he would like nothing better than to have a normal male-female relationship. Consequently, he is seldom violent, nor does he degrade his victim. He is seeking warmth, understanding, and expression of his sexual development. The victim therefore has a good chance of taking control of the situation if she does not panic. Treat this type of potential rapist as a "nice guy," showing him warmth and interest.

As in all of these hypothetical cases, the victim's objective is to pinpoint her assailant's motivations and, using an awareness of these factors, to select the proper defensive response. Since it must be done quickly, her own awareness—an informed sense of the situation—is critical.

Displaced Aggression: This individual is frustrated at work and at play, so he takes out his aggressions on the easiest target. Although this rapist does not hate women in particular, he may behave as if he does because he wishes to degrade them. He may also use physical force. This rape is usually spontaneous, not planned, and the victim can try to ameliorate the situation by getting the rapist to talk about what's bothering him (a technique that is *not* useful in dealing with other types, such as the sexual deviant, for example). Offer him coffee. Be supportive of his views. Agree that life has been cruel to him or that he has gotten a raw deal. In general, try to build rapport with him by showing how you are both in the same boat.

Woman Hater: He hates women because he feels that he has been dominated or persecuted by them most of his life: rape is his way of getting even. He therefore has a quite well-established resistance to any attempt to build rapport. He rapes frequently, and the rapes are well-planned. His acts involve degradation, humiliation and sadism. He likes to beat his victims, for instance, and may even kill them if he is frustrated. Because he selects his victims carefully, choosing only those he thinks he can dominate, a woman's own self-image and alertness are important in preventing an attack by this type of rapist.

Once this personality type has committed himself to the attack, however, deadly force will probably be required to stop him.

Sexual Deviant: This type of rapist cannot seem to control himself, and even denies that he is responsible for his acts. The psychopathology of this type can be further categorized:

The *compulsive* rapist wants to be punished, and may end the rape by murdering his victim. He is extremely dangerous because he cannot be reasoned with, and his violence can be triggered by almost anything. He also plans his attacks carefully, and is very good at fooling women. (An excellent example of this type is the Boston Strangler.) Careful preventative measures and physical force are the woman's only effective defenses since, like the woman hater, this type of rapist will not be susceptible to psychological resistance.

The *child molester* seeks gratification in sexual relations with children because he feels in control of them; in peer relationships, the molester feels inadequate. This type of rapist tends not to use force but, rather takes advantage of the child's immaturity. His actions may not progress to actual rape, but may be limited to petting and carnal knowledge. The *incestual rapist*, whether parent or other relative, is sexually excited by a member of his family. Because he also has an interest in the victim's well-being, he uses coercion rather than violence. This approach, of course, also makes it easier for him to escape detection than would the use of any form of physical abuse.

Sexually Excited Date: He does not seem to realize that he has gone beyond the limits of propriety or, by time he does, he no longer cares. He does not plan his actions and is usually repentant afterwards—but he may also deny that he was to blame. More important, he is almost never violent. He does not physically injure his victims, although he does use physical force in the sense of grappling.

Each of the above types of rapists may be further classified in terms of his prior relationship with the potential victim. He could be a boyfriend or family friend, for example. He could be an acquaintance, someone you know slightly or just by sight, either within your own neighborhood, your work area, or a regularly-attended recreation spot. The rapist could be a stranger.

Of these latter types, the stranger is the most likely to harm or murder his victim because he has no interest in her welfare. A relative, who already has a basic human relationship with his victim, would find it more difficult to commit lasting physical harm. A friend is likely to feel guilty about what he is doing, and the victim has an excellent chance of taking advantage of that guilt. Since your life is probably not in danger from someone you know, you may not wish to use deadly force to resist. This is especially true if the attacker is a brother or other relative.

Although any rapist deserves whatever violence may be committed against him, the victim in some situations may simply not wish to escalate the rape into a physical confrontation in which blindness, for example, may result. But it is also important to remember that the attacker can be motivated by more than one factor: for instance, the incestual rapist may also be a woman hater and thus, in fact, a threat to his victim's life.

Most of the suggestions given in the previous section apply to rape attacks. Here are some additional facts that women should keep in mind. *Rape is not a sex crime—it is a crime of aggression.* It is a violent act aimed at putting women in a vulnerable place than humiliating and degrading them. The rape act is used to show the attacker he is still in control or still has psychological potency. This must be kept in mind by the woman at all times. If you decide to resist, and counter attack, *do not be ladylike about it.* You will be squashing his last chance to prove he is in control or "still a man." This may mean he will go as far as he has to because it may be his last—ditch stand. If you counter attack, you *must go for broke, once started.* This of course, does not apply to the fawney pincher at the local party or the sexually excited date who goes too far for his own good.

Afterward, *call the police.* Rapists are repeaters, sometimes as many as two hundred rapes are committed by one rapist. Whether you successfully defend yourself and repel the attack or not, call the police. Think about the next time, it may be another woman, not as successful as you. The rapist may even murder next time and you could have contributed to stopping it by contacting your local police.

For assistance in preparing this chapter we are indebted to Arnold Vagts, Adjunct Professor of Psychology, Pepperdine University, and Daniel Bates, Clinical Psychologist, Department of Psychiatry and of Human Behavior, University of California at Irvine Medical Center. Both men have extensive martial arts backgrounds and are active in Shinto-Ryu karate.

Readers interested in a detailed statistical analysis of rape data are referred to the following materials, which are among the best of the numerous references available on the subject.

Amir, M., *Patterns in Forcible Rape*, Chicago: University of Chicago Press, 1971.

DSM II: Diagnostic and Statistical Manual of Mental Disorders, (Second Ed.), Washington D.C.: American Psychiatric Association, 1968.

MacDonald, J., *Rape: Offenders and Their Victims*, Springfield, Ill.: Charles C. Thomas, 1971.

Rada, R. (Ed.), *Clinical Aspects of the Rapist*, New York: Grune & Stratton, 1978.

Schultz, L. (Ed.), *Rape Victimology*, Springfield, Ill.: Charles C. Thomas, 1975.

Selkin, J., Rape, *Psychology Today*, 8 (January, 1975) 70-76.

Walker, M., & Brodsky, S.(Eds.), *Sexual Assault: The Victim and the Rapist*, Lexington, Mass.: Lexington Books, 1976.

ACKNOWLEDGEMENTS

Our special thanks go to Team Captain Carlos Cuero for patiently illustrating our Self-Defense section; to our top Black Belt competitor Doug Ivan and his Karate, Judo, Aiki-do action photos; to Senior Black belts Dan Kerr and Sgt. Potter in the Police section; Greg Oliver for his photographs; and Drs. Dan Bates and Arnold Vagts for their educated viewpoint.

KARATE STREET SURVIVAL

Fumio Demura & Dan Ivan

DAN IVAN

By Jose M. Fraguas

Daniel Ivan stood out as a glamorous and significant figure in the Japanese Martial Arts in America. An elegant and well-mannered man in an art of war, he brought the fighting style of an obscure island named Okinawa to the West. He did this by personal dedication, perseverance, and force of will. By personally choosing a few good men to spread the word with him, he became responsible for the attention the American masses paid to Japanese arts of Budo.

But Dan Ivan was far more than "just" a Karate sensei. He was a criminal investigator with the U.S. military occupation force in Japan after World War II. Ivan Sensei also was also one of the first Westerners to forget the hatred of the war and start building bridges. He did this by studying Karate with his former enemies. Ignoring the harsh words of Eastern and Western critics who questioned his openness, Ivan's strength of character and strong personal morals enabled him to forge friendships with many of the top Martial Arts masters of shattered postwar Japan. And these continued until his last day.

An example of understanding, patience, and tolerance, Dan Ivan also was humble, Charming, and knowledgeable. Moreover, he had trained directly with such notables as Isao Obata, Gogen Yamaguchi, Gozo Shioda, and Ryusho Sakagami—just to name a few. This made practitioners around the world, who would give up their first-born for 10

percent of this man's experiences, look at him with respect and envy.

A true warrior spirit, the attitude and etiquette that I admired in the old Samurai warriors since my youth, is uncommon today, not understood, and often misinterpreted. Dan Ivan epitomized the traditional values and honor that the warrior arts represent. His modesty was startlingly genuine—much like the rest of him. He was someone everybody wanted to be around. He had a level of gratitude that you don't usually see in people who teach Martial Arts.

On a rainy autumn afternoon, with a cool mist hovering above the garden that surrounded his home, Dan Ivan sat on his sofa, half reclining and with his head resting on the heel of his right hand. He spoke softly and slowly of his life and times—especially about the struggles he had when he went to Japan for the first time.

Hours later, I walked outside into a night so dark I couldn't see the keys in my hand to unlock the car. Unexpectedly, what Dan Ivan said about death and the art of facing your destiny came back to me: "Death is simply a shedding of the physical body, like the butterfly shedding its cocoon. It is a transition to a higher state of consciousness where you continue to be able to grow. Death is but a passage of life that gives meaning to our lives on earth. A true warrior knows this and embraces death as part of life…facing it with joy and tranquility. That's why the Samurai lived every single day as if it was their last."

Driving away in the darkness before the moonrise, I understood that true friends are the ones who never leave—and even if they die, they're never dead in your heart. Those who we may think of as lost friends are not dead, but gone before, advanced a stage upon the road that we'll walk some day. I smiled and realized that I had taken a little piece of Dan Ivan with me.

FUMIO DEMURA

By Jose M. Fraguas

It's been said that the truth is never pure and rarely simple. With the passing of Fumio Demura we have lost a great Sensei, a great man, and a sincere friend. He had those dual qualities so seldom seen - exuding dynamism and excitement, but at the same time an unique ability to touch people's hearts.

In his lifetime Demura Sensei was such a cheerful and invigorating presence that it was easy to forget what daunting historic tasks he set himself. As a young man, he sought to spread the art of karate in America and to educate the future generations with the ethical principles of Karate-do. These were causes hard to accomplish and heavy with risk.

Fumio Demura was too humble and honest to believe that the whole truth about him could be found on magazines, books and movies. His personality had a freshness and optimism that won support from every practitioner regardless the style – and ultimately from those that in his motherland of Japan did not root for him in the beginning of his American journey.

Demura Sensei embodied a higher goal called `the great cause of cheering us all up'. His humor often had a purpose beyond humor. In the terrible hours after one of his heart attacks, his easy jokes gave reassurance to an anxious group of friends and students concerned about him.

As a writer, publisher and karateka, I worked closely with Demura Sensei on projects for more than 30 years. We talked regularly both before and after his health issues, difficult times and joyful experiences. During all these years, I had time to reflect on what made him a great Karate-do teacher, a great Sensei, and a great friend.

Fumio Demura knew his own mind. He had firm principles – and, I believe, right ones. He expounded them clearly and acted upon them decisively in every aspect of his life.

When the world threw problems at him, he was not baffled, or disorientated, or overwhelmed. He knew almost instinctively what to do. He was vigorous, always smiling and friendly — a complete human being, concerned about other human beings who were no longer as vigorous and not quite as healthy as they used to be.

Not long time ago during a phone conversation, Demura Sensei said to me: "The importance of death, accepting it and even celebrating it is something I continue to believe in. To accept death, we have to resign ourselves as mortals to the fact that we are just a small part of a grand design." He definitely was such a big presence here on this Earth and in the art of karate-do around the world.

Demura Sensei was a force of nature. But he was more than that. He was a man filled with the joy of living. Now that his cycle in nature is complete I can still feel the emotion of entering [for the first time] in the old Santa Ana Dojo 43 years ago. His spirit lives on in each one of us who shared dojo and personal time with him.

Fumio Demura Sensei has shed his mortal skin and returned to the everlasting Tao but his legacy leaves on. He is gone but will never be forgotten.

www.ingramcontent.com/pod-product-compliance
Lightning Source LLC
Chambersburg PA
CBHW081449070526
44586CB00019B/2274